Healing Out Loud

By: Keana Shatteen

Reclaim Your Voice Power and Purpose

Copyright Page

Healing Out Loud
© 2025 Keana Shatteen

For permission requests, please contact the author at: iamkeanashatteen@gmail.com

This is a work of non-fiction based on the author's personal experiences. Names, characters, places, and events have been changed or fictionalized in some instances to protect the privacy of individuals.

First Edition: February, 2025
ISBN: 9798309258659
Printed in the United States of America

A Journey to Liberation

Hey Soulmate!

Welcome to Healing Out Loud! As you open these pages, you're not just beginning a book—you're embarking on a deeply personal and transformative journey. Healing is a word we often hear but rarely explore in its entirety. We hear phrases like, "time heals all wounds," but if you've experienced profound loss or mental and emotional struggles, you know that isn't the full truth. Time alone does not heal. Time can soften the sharp edges, but true healing—true liberation—requires more. It asks us to meet ourselves fully: mentally, emotionally, physically, and spiritually.

Healing is not about going back to how things used to be. It's about moving forward, even when it feels impossible. Moving forward means embracing the uncertainty of what's ahead, like stepping into a room filled with darkness but trusting that the light switch is within reach. For example, after losing a job you poured your heart into, moving forward might look like pursuing a passion you've put on hold, discovering a new skill, or finding a career path that aligns more deeply with your values. It's about shedding the weight of expectations, releasing the pain we've carried, and stepping boldly into what could be. Liberation lies in recognizing that we can transform our wounds into wisdom, our pain into purpose, and our silence into strength.

This book is about healing out loud—about voicing the mental and emotional pain, loss, and transformation we often keep hidden. Loss is not just about death; it's the loss of a dream, like starting a business that didn't succeed, a job we poured our hearts into only to face an unexpected layoff, a relationship we thought would last but didn't, or even letting go of a version of ourselves we no longer recognize when life demands change. These losses disrupt our emotional balance and mental well-being, leaving us feeling unsteady and disconnected from who we truly are.

Healing goes beyond mere survival; it's about transformation. It's about restoring balance in every aspect of our lives—mentally, emotionally, physically, and spiritually. Healing involves working through the weight of loss and the emotional upheaval it brings to find a way to realign with our inner selves. Liberation isn't about forgetting what happened; it's about integrating the pain into the story of who we are becoming.

When we endure emotional and mental pain, it disrupts the flow of our energy. Healing restores that flow—helping us move from pain to empowerment. It's about using those experiences as catalysts for transformation and addressing the imbalances in our mental, emotional, and physical lives to reclaim our sense of self.

Healing isn't instantaneous or linear. It requires patience, persistence, and a willingness to embrace mental discomfort and vulnerability. True growth occurs when we intentionally lean into discomfort, honor our emotions, and prioritize our well-being as we realign ourselves on every level.

This book doesn't shy away from acknowledging the pain of mental and emotional wounds — but it also celebrates the hope that healing brings. Every loss, whether it's the end of a relationship, a job, a dream, or even a past self, creates space for new beginnings. Healing isn't about recovering what was lost; it's about discovering what can emerge from the ashes.

Liberation requires courage. It asks us to let go of what's been keeping us small and to embrace the truth of who we are, even when it feels uncomfortable. You don't need to have all the answers to begin this journey. You don't need to know exactly how everything will unfold. What matters is that you take the first step, even when you're unsure, even when it feels like the world is falling apart around you.

This book isn't just about survival — it's about what comes after the loss. It's about how we rebuild and rediscover ourselves, mentally, emotionally, and spiritually. It's about healing out loud, finding strength in vulnerability, and allowing ourselves to be transformed by the process. It's about restoring balance, clarity, and emotional stability in all aspects of our lives.

I don't have all the answers, but I've learned that healing isn't about having a clear path. It's about taking the journey, one step at a time, even when the way forward is uncertain. Each chapter of loss sets the stage for something new — a more empowered, aligned version of ourselves, shaped by the wisdom that can only come from walking through the fire.

Endings are painful, but they also bring the possibility of new beginnings. My healing journey has been, and continues to be, an ongoing process of rediscovery — of finding balance within myself, mind, body, and spirit. I've learned that liberation isn't just personal — it's universal. When we heal, we create ripples of change that touch the lives of others. By sharing our stories and reclaiming our voices, we inspire others to do the same.

I invite you to join me on this journey. Together, let's commit to healing out loud, to moving through our pain with grace and courage, and to emerging as the most liberated versions of ourselves. Let's honor every crack and imperfection as evidence of our strength, and trust that each painful ending is also a new beginning.

With love and gratitude,

Keana

Table of Contents

Introduction
- A Journey to Liberation

Preparation
- Trigger Warnings and Professional Disclaimer
- Mental Health Resources

The Journey Begins
- Prologue
- Key Moments of Loss and Growth

Healing and Reflection
- Reclaiming My Voice
- A New Perspective on Love
- Embracing Growth

Interactive Tools for Healing
- Timeline and Practical Exercises

Cultural Context and Systemic Barriers
- Navigating Mental Health as a Black Woman
- Overcoming Systemic Challenges

Looking Ahead
- The Aligned Liberation Philosophy

Additional Resources
- Reader's Guide
- Glossary of Terms
- Resources Section

Closing
- Acknowledgments
- About the Author

Trigger Warnings

Before you dive deeper into this book, I want to offer a gentle reminder that the pages ahead cover sensitive topics, including depression, anxiety, suicide, self-harm, and trauma. If you've experienced any of these struggles, please take care of yourself as you read. If the content becomes overwhelming, it's okay to step away, take a break, or reach out to someone for support. Prioritize your mental and emotional well-being above all else.

Professional Disclaimer

The stories and insights in this book are drawn from my personal experiences. While I hope they offer you encouragement and comfort, this book is not a replacement for professional medical or psychological advice. If you are experiencing mental health challenges, I encourage you to seek help from a licensed therapist, counselor, or mental health professional who can provide the care and guidance tailored to your unique situation.

Mental Health Resources

If, at any point, you feel like you need immediate support, please know there are resources available to help:

- **988 Suicide & Crisis Lifeline**: Dial 988 (24/7 support for those in crisis or needing immediate mental health assistance)
- **Crisis Text Line**: Text HOME to 741741 (24/7 confidential text support)
- **National Alliance on Mental Illness (NAMI) Helpline**: 1-800-950-NAMI (6264) or text NAMI to 741741 (Free information and support for mental health conditions)
- **American Foundation for Suicide Prevention (AFSP)**: afsp.org (Resources, education, and support for suicide prevention)
- **Substance Abuse and Mental Health Services Administration (SAMHSA) National Helpline**: 1-800-662-HELP (4357) (Free, confidential help for individuals facing mental health or substance use issues)
- **The Trevor Project**: 1-866-488-7386 or text START to 678678 (Crisis intervention and suicide prevention for LGBTQIA+ youth)

Please refer to the full list of resources at the end of the book for further support options. Thank you for trusting me with your time and heart. Let's begin this journey together.

Prologue

Shattered Reflections

"Every step I take, no matter how small, leads me closer to healing."

The harsh fluorescent lights of the hospital room buzzed overhead, their unforgiving glare exposing every raw emotion I had tried so hard to bury. As I blinked my eyes open, struggling to adjust, the room slowly came into focus. The steady beep of machines echoed around me, grounding me in the reality of where I was—and why.

I was alive.

That realization hit me hard. It wasn't relief that filled me but a mix of confusion, disappointment, and exhaustion. Hours before—or was it days? —I had swallowed a deadly combination of pills and wine, desperate to silence the chaos in my mind. But here I was, alive, with the weight of my actions pressing down on me like a lead blanket. The drugs still coursed through my body, leaving me sluggish and disconnected from the world around me.

Before I had taken the pills, I had sent my husband a final text: "Thanks for not throwing away my pills." It wasn't a clear goodbye, but it was enough. A part of me had wanted him to stop me. To intervene, like he had done before. But this time, no one stopped me. No one had come between me and the escape I thought I wanted.

And now, here I was.

As I lay there, my thoughts jumbled, memories of that day began to flood back. The Easter argument—how heated it had become. The hurt that lingered between us, unresolved. The police knocking on the patio door, my dog barking uncontrollably, my aunt rushing in after. It felt like the world had collapsed in on itself, and I had been left with no way out.

To my left, my aunt sat quietly, her face etched with concern and a quiet relief that I didn't feel worthy of. She had been there for me, rushing to the hospital the moment she knew, her presence grounding me in ways I wasn't sure I deserved. Across the room, my wusband stood with arms crossed, his expression a storm of anger and confusion. We had fought bitterly the day before — he had known about my struggles, had seen me at my lowest. But we hadn't bridged the gap between us, hadn't dealt with the darkness that had been quietly growing inside me. Now, the aftermath of that fight hung in the air between us, thick and suffocating.

"Why?" he asked, his voice low but trembling with emotions he was trying to contain. "Why did you do this?"

I couldn't meet his gaze. The shame was too heavy, too overwhelming. "You knew how much I was struggling," I whispered, my voice barely audible. "But you still… you still left the pills where I could find them."

His face hardened, frustration flaring in his eyes. "You think this is my fault?" His voice cracked with restrained anger. "I didn't make you take them."

Tears filled my eyes, blurring the already sterile surroundings. "I just wanted the pain to stop," I choked out. "I didn't know what else to do."

The silence that followed was thick and unbearable. Every word we spoke felt like a stab, deepening the divide between us. I wanted to explain, to make him understand the depth of my despair, but the words wouldn't come. I was drowning in shame — shame for what I had done, shame for the damage I had caused.

My thoughts drifted to my son, his innocent face flashing before me. The thought of him ripped through me like a dagger. How could I have almost left him? How could I have been so selfish, so consumed by my own pain that I didn't think of him? He deserved better — a mother who could fight through the darkness, who could find a way forward, even when it felt impossible.

In that moment, I realized that this battle wasn't just mine — it was his too. My son needed me, and I had almost taken myself from him. I had come so close to leaving him without a mother, subjecting him to the same pain I had carried when I lost my own mother. How had I let it come to this?
"We can't keep going like this," my wusband said finally, his voice breaking the silence that had settled like a heavy fog. "Something has to change."
"I know," I whispered, the weight of his words settling over me. "I know."

We sat in that heavy silence, both lost in our own thoughts, both grappling with the enormity of what had just happened. The tension between us was thick, the pain and anger swirling together in ways neither of us knew how to address. I wanted to fix it, wanted to say something that would make it all better, but I didn't have the words. I didn't even know if words could fix this.

As my wusband stood up and walked to the door, saying he needed some air, a wave of loneliness washed over me. I had come so close to ending everything, to walking away from all of it, but now I was still here. Still breathing. Still alive. And as I lay there, feeling the heaviness of the hospital room press in on me, I realized something: this wasn't the end. It couldn't be.

I made a quiet promise to myself in that moment. I didn't know how I would do it, and I didn't know if I had the strength to follow through, but I would try. I would try to heal. I would try to find my way out of the darkness, one small step at a time. Not just for myself, but for my son, for the people who loved me, for the life I had almost thrown away.

This was my turning point. My rock bottom. But it was also the beginning of something new. The journey ahead would be long, difficult, and filled with challenges I couldn't yet foresee, but I knew one thing for sure: I had been given a second chance, and I owed it to myself, to my son, to fight for it.

As I lay there, exhausted and overwhelmed, I clung to one thought: This is not the end of my story. It's just the beginning of a new chapter- one of healing, growth, and rediscovery. One step at a time, I would find my way back to life. Back to hope. Back to the person, the mother, I knew I could be.

Chapter 1
The Beginning of the End

"Healing begins with understanding and accepting our deepest wounds."

I was sixteen when my world shattered, the age when most teenagers are dreaming of freedom and the future. Instead, I found myself facing a loss so profound it would alter the course of my life forever. My mom's death was sudden and brutal, a swift and unexpected blow that left me gasping for air, struggling to make sense of a world that no longer included her.

She was only forty-three when an aneurysm resulted in a massive heart attack, stealing her away from me in the blink of an eye. Forty-three - an age that had once seemed so distant to my teenage self, now feels tragically young. We had been so close, our relationship bordering on codependency, a bond so tight that losing her felt like losing a vital part of myself. One moment, she was there—my rock, my confidante, my everything—and the next, she was gone, leaving behind a void so vast and empty I couldn't fathom how to begin filling it.

That fateful Sunday morning started like any other, deceptively ordinary. The air was filled with the scent of coffee and the soft rustle of newspaper pages - sounds that would forever remind me of lazy weekends with Mom. She had just finished her shower and called me to help blow dry her hair, a routine we'd shared countless times before. As I gently ran the dryer through her damp locks, I noticed her wincing, her hand moving to her chest more frequently than usual.

"Mom, what's wrong?" I asked, unable to mask the concern in my voice. The pit in my stomach grew as I watched her face contorted with pain.

She tried to smile, to reassure me as she always did, but her voice betrayed her fear. "It's just a little discomfort, sweetheart," she said, but her shallow breathing and the way she clutched at her chest told a different story. The pain seemed to intensify with each passing moment, and I felt a rising panic, a premonition that this was more than just a passing discomfort.

What followed next was a blur of frantic activity. I remember calling for help, my trembling fingers barely able to dial the numbers. The paramedics arrived in what seemed like seconds and an eternity all at once. They moved with practiced efficiency, their calm professionalism a stark contrast to the chaos I felt inside. I watched, helpless, as they loaded my mother onto a stretcher, her face pale and drawn with pain. As they prepared to take her away, she looked at me and said, "Keana, grab my purse." It was the last thing she asked of me, and I held onto it tightly, as if it were the last connection I had to her.

I followed them outside; my feet unsteady on the pavement. As the ambulance drove away, its sirens piercing the quiet Sunday morning, I felt rooted to the spot. The sound of the sirens faded into the distance, and it was at that moment, standing there in the middle of the street, with my mother's purse held tightly in my hands, that I felt the last threads of my childhood innocence unravel. I wasn't just a sixteen-year-old girl anymore. I was someone standing on the edge of an abyss about to fall into a new, harsher reality I didn't want to face.

The hospital waiting room was a purgatory of harsh fluorescent lights and hushed voices. Time lost all meaning as I sat there, my hands clasped so tightly my knuckles turned white. Every time the double doors swung open, I felt my heart leap, hoping for good news, dreading the worst. The sterile smell of disinfectant, the squeaking of nurses' shoes on linoleum floors, the muted beeping of distant machines - these sensations would be forever etched in my memory, a backdrop to the most pivotal moment of my young life.

When the doctor finally approached, his face grave and his steps measured, I felt a cold dread settle in my stomach. Time seemed to slow as he neared, and I found myself wishing I could freeze this moment, to live forever in this state of unknowing rather than face the truth I saw written in his eyes.

"I'm sorry," he said, his voice gentle but firm. "We did everything we could, but your mother didn't make it."

The words hit me like a physical blow. I remember shaking my head, denial rising like a tide. "No," I said, my voice breaking. "She can't be gone. She can't be!" But she was, and in that moment, a part of me died too.

The days that followed were a blur of grief and disbelief. Our home, once warm and filled with her laughter, felt hollow. Her absence was a tangible thing, pressing in on me from all sides. I found myself wandering into her room, breathing in her lingering scent, desperately trying to hold onto any trace of her.

Nights were the hardest. I'd been used to sleeping in her bed, finding comfort in her presence. Now, I lay awake in her room, the silence deafening, the emptiness overwhelming. I'd reach out in the darkness, half-expecting to feel her warmth, only to be met with cold sheets and the crushing reality of her absence.

My relationship with my mother had been the cornerstone of my existence. We were more than just mother and daughter; we were best friends, confidantes, each other's support system. She was the one who encouraged my dreams, who believed in me unconditionally, who taught me what it meant to be loved and to love in return. Her loss left a gaping hole in my life, a void that I didn't know how to fill.

The contrast between my relationship with my mother and my father was stark and painful. While my mother had been my rock, my father was more like shifting sand, unreliable and distant. Before their separation, he had been physically present but emotionally absent, his struggle with alcoholism creating a barrier between us that seemed insurmountable.

I remember the tension that would fill our home when he'd had too much to drink, the way my mother's smile would tighten, the way I'd make myself small, trying to avoid his notice. There were fleeting moments of connection - a shared laugh over a TV show, a rare sober conversation about school - but these were always overshadowed by the chaos his addiction brought into our lives.

After the separation, even his physical presence became scarce. He moved away, and his drinking worsened. The emotional chasm between us grew wider, deeper. Phone calls became less frequent, visits rarer still. Each time I saw him, he seemed a little more distant, a little less like the father I desperately wanted him to be.

It was my mother who stepped in to fill the void he left, becoming both mom and dad, provider and nurturer. She worked tirelessly to create stability in our home, to shield me from the harsh realities of our situation. Her love was a constant, unwavering force in my life, a stark contrast to the unpredictability of my father's affection.

Losing her felt like losing my only lifeline in a turbulent sea. The fear of abandonment, which had taken root with my father's emotional absence, now blossomed into full-blown terror. If I could lose my mother - the one person who had always been there for me - what guarantee did I have that anyone else would stay?

The pain of her loss was unlike anything I had ever experienced or could have imagined. It was a physical ache, a heaviness in my chest that made it hard to breathe. There were moments when the grief was so overwhelming that I wasn't sure how I would survive it. But somehow, I did. Each day, I found the strength to get out of bed, to go through the motions of living, even when it felt impossible.

Looking back now, I realize that my mother's death, as devastating as it was, also marked the beginning of a journey - a difficult, often painful journey of self-discovery and resilience. It forced me to confront emotions and situations that most of my peers couldn't even imagine. It pushed me to find strength within myself that I didn't know I possessed.

In the years that followed, this loss would shape every aspect of my life - my relationships, my sense of self-worth, my ability to trust and be vulnerable. The shadow of my mother's death loomed large, influencing decisions both big and small. It made me both more guarded and more desperate for connection, a contradiction that would lead me down paths both healing and harmful.

If I could go back and speak to my sixteen-year-old self, standing shellshocked in that hospital waiting room, I would have so much to say. I would tell her that she is stronger than she knows that the pain she feels, as all-consuming as it is, will not defeat her. I would tell her that she is worthy of love and respect, that her trauma does not define her.

I would urge her to seek help, to not suffer in silence. I would encourage her to lean on friends and family, to find a counselor who could help her navigate the tumultuous waters of grief. I would remind her that it's okay to cry, to scream, to feel angry at the unfairness of it all - but it's also okay to laugh, to find moments of joy, to keep living.

Most importantly, I would tell her that healing is a journey, not a destination. That it's okay to take it one step at a time, to have days when it feels like she's moving backward instead of forward. I would assure her that one day, she will be able to think of her mother and smile through the tears, to feel gratitude for the time they had together alongside the pain of what was lost.

The path ahead would be long and often difficult, fraught with challenges and setbacks. But it would also be a path of growth, of self-discovery, of learning to love and be loved again. The scars from those years would remain, but they would become testaments to my strength, my resilience, my ability to survive even the darkest of times.

My mother's death was the end of one chapter of my life, but it was also the beginning of another. It was the catalyst that would shape me into the person I am today - someone who understands the depths of loss, but also the heights of love; someone who knows the value of compassion and the strength it takes to keep going when all seems lost.

In the end, I've come to understand that the greatest tribute I can pay to my mother is not just to survive in her absence, but to truly live - to love deeply, to pursue my dreams, to find joy in the world around me. It's a journey I'm still on, one step at a time, carrying her memory with me always.

Reflection Questions

1. How do you cope with significant losses in your life? Have you experienced a loss that fundamentally changed your perspective?

2. What memories of loved ones have been most impactful for you? How do these memories shape your current relationships and outlook on life?

3. How do you practice self-love and self-compassion during times of grief or trauma? What strategies have you found most helpful?

4. If you could speak to your younger self during a difficult time, what advice or comfort would you offer?

5. How has your relationship with your parents (or guardians) influenced your ability to form and maintain other relationships in your life?

Tips for Healing

1. Allow Yourself to Grieve: Grieving is a natural and necessary process. Give yourself permission to feel and express your emotions without judgment. There's no "right" way to grieve, and no set timeline for healing.

2. Seek Support Systems: Connect with friends, family, or support groups who can offer comfort and understanding. Don't be afraid to lean on others during difficult times. Professional help, such as therapy or counseling, can also be invaluable in navigating complex emotions.

3. Create a Memory Journal: Document your memories and feelings to help process your grief and keep your loved one's memory alive. This can be a

therapeutic way to work through your emotions and preserve precious memories.

4. Practice Self-Care: Prioritize your physical and emotional well-being. This might include regular exercise, maintaining a healthy diet, getting enough sleep, or engaging in activities that bring you joy and relaxation.

5. Establish New Routines: While it's important to honor the past, creating new routines can help you move forward. This might involve taking up a new hobby, volunteering, or establishing new traditions that give your life structure and purpose.

Healing Activity: Letter to Your Younger Self

Take some time to write a letter to your younger self, particularly focusing on a challenging period in your life. What wisdom would you share? What comfort would you offer? What strengths would you remind yourself of? This exercise can help you reflect on your growth, acknowledge your resilience, and practice self-compassion.

Understanding Grief: A Brief Overview

Grief is a complex and deeply personal experience that can affect us in many ways. While often associated with death, we can grieve many types of losses - the end of a relationship, the loss of a job, or even the loss of a dream or expectation. Elisabeth Kübler-Ross's Five Stages of Grief (denial, anger, bargaining, depression, and acceptance) are widely known, but it's important to remember that grief isn't linear. People may experience these stages in different orders, revisit stages multiple times, or experience additional emotions not captured in this model. Recent grief research emphasizes that healthy grieving often involves maintaining a connection with the deceased while also finding ways to continue living and finding new meaning. This concept, known as "continuing bonds," suggests that the goal of grief isn't to "get over" the loss, but to find a new way of maintaining a relationship with the person who has died while also engaging fully in life.

Remember, there's no "right" way to grieve. Your journey is unique to you, and it's okay to seek help if you're struggling. Professional support, such as grief counseling, can provide valuable tools and strategies for navigating the complex emotions that come with loss.

As we move forward in this book, remember that healing is a journey, not a destination. Each chapter of our lives, even the painful ones, contributes to who we are. By sharing our stories, reflecting on our experiences, and supporting each other, we can find strength, resilience, and hope, even in the face of profound loss.

Chapter 2
A Desperate Search for Solace

"Healing means taking a step back to regain your strength and step forward with resilience."

In the aftermath of my mother's death, the world became a landscape of shadows and sharp edges. Every familiar place, every routine, was now tainted by her absence. I was sent to live with my aunt and cousin, a well-intentioned arrangement that felt more like exile than comfort. My father, still grappling with his own demons of alcoholism, wasn't an option. He was living in a small apartment with his brother, my uncle, his life a tumultuous sea of addiction that offered no safe harbor for a grieving teenager. I want to be clear—my feeling of exile wasn't meant as any disrespect to my aunt or cousin.

My aunt tried her best to provide a stable environment, and they welcomed me with open arms, but the hole left by my mother's passing was too vast, too raw to be filled by anyone else. Despite their efforts, their home never felt like my home. The feeling of "home," I realized, had faded the day my mother stopped breathing. It was as if the very concept had died along with her, leaving me adrift in a world that suddenly seemed vast and terrifyingly empty.

It was in this state of profound emptiness and loneliness that I met my high school sweetheart, just two months after my mother's passing. At first, his attention felt like a lifeline, a connection to something outside of my grief. He was charming and attentive, and his interest in me was like a balm to my wounded soul. In my desperate attempt to find solace and cling to anything that would make the pain more bearable, I threw myself into the relationship with the reckless abandon of someone drowning, reaching for any floating debris.

I wanted so badly to feel loved and valued again, to fill the void in my heart left by my mother's death. The intensity of my need for connection blinded me to the red flags that, in retrospect, were waving furiously from the very beginning. But when you're standing in the dark, any light seems bright, no matter how artificial or dangerous it might be.

At first, things seemed to be going well. He was there for me, offering a shoulder to cry on and an ear to listen. His presence felt like a shield against the overwhelming grief and loneliness that threatened to consume me. For a brief time, I felt like maybe, just maybe, I could find a way to be okay again.

But as time went on, the relationship began to twist into something dark and painful. What started as a source of comfort soon became a source of confusion and fear. His attention turned possessive, his charm giving way to criticism and anger. The boy who had once seemed like my savior was slowly revealing himself to be my tormentor.

One particular incident stands out sharply in my memory. We were driving home after an argument, and he became furious when I refused to let him keep my car. His temper exploded, and in a violent rage, he ripped the sun visor off the passenger side. As if that wasn't enough, he then began hitting me repeatedly on the right side of my face — the side visible to him. It was at that moment that someone in another car noticed what was happening and started to trail us, as if they wanted to intervene. But I eventually lost them in traffic, leaving me alone to endure the rest of the ride with my boyfriend's fists continuing to land on my face.

I remember gripping the steering wheel tightly, my heart racing, tears welling up in my eyes. I wanted to disappear, to be anywhere but there. But a part of me also wanted to stay, to fix things, to make him happy again. That's how it starts — small moments of discomfort that you brush aside, making excuses for the person you care about.

That incident should have been my wake-up call, the moment I walked away for good. But leaving an abusive relationship is rarely that simple. The cycle of abuse and reconciliation, the fear of being alone, and my own diminished self-esteem kept me trapped for far too long.

By the time we arrived, my face was so bruised that I was afraid to let anyone see me. I hid out at my cousin's house for that entire week during spring break, using makeup and my hair to cover the evidence of his abuse. I covered my beaten face and bruised eye, telling myself I just needed to get through it.

Around this time, Eve's song "Love is Blind" was released, and it felt like the song was speaking directly to my experience. The lyrics described how love — or the illusion of it — could blind someone to the pain and violence they were enduring. Even though I heard the lyrics, I never imagined that somehow this could have been me. Hearing the song helped me realize that the abuse I was suffering wasn't normal or deserved, and that staying in the relationship was destroying me, not saving me.

As the weeks turned into months, these incidents became more frequent, more intense. The yelling turned into grabbing, the insults became more personal and cutting. After each outburst, he would apologize profusely, showering me with affection and promises that it would never happen again. And I, still reeling from the loss of my mother and desperate for any form of love and connection, would believe him.

There were good times too, moments when he was the caring, attentive boyfriend I craved. These glimpses of tenderness made it harder to see the relationship for what it truly was — abusive and damaging. I clung to these positive moments, using them to justify staying, even as the bad times began to outnumber the good.

My family knew about one incident of abuse — an ugly fight that had escalated beyond control. I was so embarrassed by it that, when they found out, I felt ashamed. That shame silenced me, and I never told them about the other incidents. I downplayed the severity, telling them it was a one-time thing, an isolated incident. But the truth was that there were many other times I kept hidden, burying the pain deep inside and pretending everything was fine.

On the surface, I tried to maintain a semblance of normalcy, but inside, I was crumbling. The constant fear and anxiety took a toll on my mental and physical health, leaving me feeling even more isolated and alone. My self-esteem plummeted, and I felt trapped in a cycle of pain and degradation.

The abusive relationship reinforced my belief that I was unlovable and destined to suffer. There were moments when I wanted to leave, to escape the abuse and find a way to heal. But the thought of being alone again, of facing the void without even the illusion of love and support, was terrifying. I convinced myself that I needed him, that I couldn't survive without him, even though staying with him was slowly destroying me.

In the months leading up to my high school graduation, I began to gather the strength to end the relationship. This time marked the end of a painful chapter in my life and the beginning of an uncertain future. I knew that I deserved better, that I needed to break free from the cycle of abuse and ready myself for a fresh start. Leaving him was a significant step, but it was only the beginning of a long journey toward healing and self-discovery.

As I reflect on this period of my life, I realize that my relationship with him was a manifestation of my unresolved grief and trauma. I sought solace in someone who mirrored the dysfunction I had known, believing that was all I deserved. But through the pain and the struggle, I began to understand the importance of self-love and the need to seek support.

Breaking free from his abuse was a turning point in my life. It taught me that healing is possible, even in the darkest of times. It showed me the strength I had within myself—a strength that had been buried beneath layers of pain and self-doubt. This experience, as painful as it was, became a crucial step in my journey toward understanding my worth and reclaiming my power.

Reflection Questions

1. Have you ever been in a relationship that felt both comforting and damaging? How did you navigate the conflicting emotions?
2. What are some red flags in relationships that you now recognize but might have overlooked in the past?
3. How has your experience with loss or trauma influenced your relationships? In what ways have you seen patterns repeat or change?
4. What does self-love mean to you, and how do you practice it in your relationships?
5. If you could send a message to someone currently in an abusive relationship, what would you say to support and encourage them?

Tips for Healing

1. Recognize Red Flags: Pay attention to behaviors that make you feel uncomfortable or unsafe. Trust your instincts - if something feels wrong, it probably is.

2. Focus on Self-Love: Practice self-love and self-compassion before seeking validation from others. Be kind to yourself as you heal. Remember that the abuse was not your fault, and recovery takes time.

3. Establish Boundaries: Learn to establish clear boundaries to protect your emotional health during vulnerable times. and maintain healthy boundaries in all your relationships. It's okay to say no and to prioritize your well-being.

4. Seek Professional Help: Therapy can provide tools and support for healing from abusive relationships and addressing underlying traumas.

Healing Activity: Self-Worth Affirmations

Create a list of positive affirmations that reinforce your self-worth. Write them down and read them aloud to yourself daily. Some examples might include:

- I am worthy of love and respect.

- My feelings and needs are valid.

- I trust my own judgment.

- I have the strength to create positive change in my life.

- I deserve to be treated with kindness and compassion.

Understanding Abusive Relationships: Breaking the Cycle

Abusive relationships often follow a cycle that can be difficult to recognize when you're in it. This cycle typically includes three phases:

1. Tension Building: The abuser becomes increasingly irritable, communicative, and tense. The victim often feels like they're "walking on eggshells."

2. Acute Violence: The tension leads to an abusive incident, which can be physical, emotional, or both.

3. Reconciliation/"Honeymoon": The abuser apologizes, shows remorse, and may promise it will never happen again. They might be extra attentive and loving during this phase.

Understanding this cycle can help individuals recognize patterns in their own relationships. It's important to note that not all abusive relationships follow this exact pattern, and emotional abuse can be just as damaging as physical abuse.

Factors that often keep people in abusive relationships include:

- Fear of the abuser
- Low self-esteem
- Financial dependence
- Cultural or religious beliefs
- Hope that the abuser will change
- Isolation from friends and family

Breaking free from an abusive relationship is a process that often requires support and careful planning. If you or someone you know is in an abusive relationship, remember that help is available. National domestic violence hotlines can provide resources, support, and safety planning assistance.

Remember, everyone deserves to be in a relationship based on mutual respect, trust, and support. Healing from abuse is possible, and with time and support, survivors can reclaim their power and build healthy, fulfilling relationships.

As we close this chapter, remember that your past experiences do not define your future. Each day is an opportunity to choose self-love, to set healthy boundaries, and to surround yourself with people who truly value and respect you. Your journey of healing and self-discovery is unique, and every step you take towards a healthier, happier you is a victory worth celebrating.

Chapter 3
New Beginnings Old Patterns

"True healing starts when we stop running from our past and start embracing our journey."

Stepping onto the college campus felt like entering a new world, a place brimming with possibility and the promise of a fresh start. I was ready for a change after high school. Going away to college wasn't just about academics; it was my way of escaping my past. I needed to start somewhere new, somewhere I didn't know anyone and didn't have to risk seeing my ex. I was desperate for a place where I could start fresh, leave behind the painful memories, and redefine myself.

The sprawling grounds, the diverse faces, the palpable energy of academic pursuit—it was all at once exhilarating and terrifying. For the first time since my mother's death, I felt a flicker of hope, a tentative belief that perhaps I could redefine myself, shed the weight of my past, and become someone new.

The first few weeks were a whirlwind of orientation activities, new faces, and the challenge of navigating campus life. I threw myself into it all with desperate enthusiasm, determined to keep busy, to outrun the lingering shadows of grief and trauma that still clung to me like a second skin. But in the quiet moments, alone in my dorm room, the memories would creep back in. The loss of my mother, the scars from my abusive relationship — they were still there, just beneath the surface, waiting for moments of stillness to resurface.

One Sunday morning in my freshman year, I woke up in tears. I hadn't been dreaming, yet the grief hit me like a wave as soon as my eyes opened. I felt the overwhelming sense of loss wash over me, and all I could do was lie there, sobbing, as the pain of missing my mother became too much to bear. It was as though I had been running for so long, and in that moment, the grief had finally caught up to me. The new environment, the distractions, the busy schedules — none of it could shield me from the reality of her absence. That morning reminded me that no matter where I went or how hard I tried to escape, the grief would always be there, waiting for me.

Emotionally, I had tried to bury my grief under layers of distraction, hoping that new experiences would eventually erase the pain. But I learned that grief doesn't just disappear because you're in a new environment. It lingers, showing up in unexpected ways — like in the sleepless nights, the constant anxiety, or the physical exhaustion that seemed to hang over me. I hadn't yet realized that healing required me to confront the pain rather than avoid it. Instead, I was using busyness as a way to outrun my emotions.

Financial aid and part-time jobs helped me get by, but there was always an underlying current of struggle and loneliness.

My dad, still battling his own demons of alcoholism, remained a distant figure, unable to provide the support — emotional or financial — that I so desperately needed. This reality added another layer of pressure to my college experience, a constant reminder of the adult responsibilities I had to shoulder alongside my studies.

After my abusive high school relationship ended, I didn't have any real or meaningful romantic connections. My interactions were limited to casual hookups, none of which filled the void left by my past traumas. These encounters, while temporarily distracting, often left me feeling more empty and disconnected than before. I was chasing temporary fixes, thinking they could heal the deeper wounds, but all they did was highlight how lost I truly felt.

It was during my sophomore year, at the beginning of the fall semester, when I unexpectedly crossed paths with the man who would later become my "wusband" (was my wusband) — a term of endearment I now use for my wusband. I had first noticed him during my freshman year, but it wasn't until we shared a work-study assignment that we began to speak. His presence intrigued me from the start.

There was an ease about him, a genuineness that stood in stark contrast to the tumultuous relationships I had known. I remember it clearly: it was a warm afternoon, and I was walking through the quad when I saw him sitting at a table, casually eating lunch. He was mid-bite, about to eat a fry, when a piece fell from his mouth and landed on the table. Without thinking, I walked up to him and asked, "How was your summer?"

It wasn't a planned encounter, but the conversation flowed easily, and for the first time in a long while, I felt comfortable approaching someone. He seemed relaxed, grounded, and genuinely interested in our casual conversation about the summer, classes, and how overwhelming the start of the year had been. There was no pressure, no awkwardness, just two people talking, sharing the same space on a sunny day.

It felt good to have a lighthearted moment amidst the heaviness I had been carrying.

I didn't think much of it after that day. We'd spoken, and that was that. It wasn't until a couple of weeks later that I learned he and I would be working together tutoring city youth after school. Our work-study assignments had brought us together again, and it was in those tutoring sessions that our connection deepened.

As we worked side by side, helping kids with their homework, we started talking more—about life, our classes, and eventually, about things that mattered. I found myself drawn to his attentiveness and care. He listened when I spoke—really listened—in a way that made me feel seen and valued. After the volatility of my previous relationship, his calm demeanor felt like a safe harbor. I could feel a sense of lightness around him, something that had been missing from my life for so long. For the first time since my mother's death, I felt like I could exhale.

However, there was a complicated layer to our relationship that I tried to overlook. He had been in a relationship with another girl when we met. Initially, he assured me that things were ending between them, but the reality was more tangled. As we grew closer, I discovered that he was still involved with her, creating a web of deceit that cast a shadow over our budding romance.

Despite the moral conflict and the guilt I felt, I continued to date him throughout college. The fear of being alone and the comfort I found in his presence outweighed my reservations. We spent nearly every moment together, and he became my anchor in the storm of college life. I rationalized it by focusing on the positive aspects of our time together. Different from my past experiences, there was no abuse, no fear. Instead, there was love, companionship, and a sense of partnership that I desperately needed.

Looking back, I can see how my lack of self-worth and unresolved traumas influenced my decisions. I sought validation and love outside myself, not understanding that true acceptance had to come from within. This relationship, while providing comfort and companionship, was also enabling me to avoid confronting my deeper issues. I was using this relationship as a distraction, much like I had used casual hookups and busyness before. I was still running from myself, afraid to face the emotional wounds that needed healing.

Had I already developed a healthy view of self-love, I might not have found myself in a situation where I was willing to accept a relationship that started with deceit. A strong sense of self-worth would have made me seek relationships built on mutual respect and integrity from the start. If I had been taught to expect respect from men, his respect would have been a given rather than a rare and treasured exception. I would have seen it as a baseline requirement for any relationship rather than a unique reason to stay.

Yet, even as I recognized these patterns, I struggled to break free from them. The comfort and security I felt with my "wusband" were real, and the thought of losing that was terrifying. So I stayed, balancing on the edge of a relationship that was neither fully honest nor entirely dishonest, trying to convince myself that this gray area was where I belonged.

Looking back on this time, I realize that it was a crucial chapter in my ongoing journey of self-discovery and healing. It was during these years that I began to understand the depth of my wounds and the work I would need to do to truly heal. While I wasn't yet ready to fully confront all of my issues, the seeds of self-awareness and change were being planted.

This chapter of my life, with all its complications and contradictions, was a necessary step in my path toward understanding myself and my needs in relationships. It set the stage for the growth and self-reflection that would come later, teaching me that true healing begins not when we find the perfect relationship, but when we start to honestly examine ourselves and our patterns.

Reflection Questions

1. What recurring patterns do you notice in your relationships and how have these patterns impacted your growth?

2. Have you ever compromised your values or overlooked red flags in a relationship out of fear of being alone? How did this impact you?

3. What does a healthy, respectful relationship look like to you? How has this vision evolved as you've grown and had different experiences?

4. In what ways do you seek validation from others? How might you work on finding that validation within yourself instead?

5. How do you balance the desire for companionship with the need for personal growth and self-discovery?

Tips for Healing:

1. Practice Self-Reflection: Regularly take time to examine your thoughts, feelings, and behaviors in relationships. Journaling can be a helpful tool for this.

2. Embrace Change: Be open to new ways of thinking and behaving in relationships.

3. Set Healthy Boundaries: Protect your peace by establishing clear emotional boundaries.

4. Celebrate Progress: Every step forward is a victory, even if progress feels slow.

5. Seek Support: Don't hesitate to reach out to friends, family, or a therapist when you need help processing your experiences or making difficult decisions.

6. Embrace Growth: View each relationship, even challenging ones, as opportunities for learning and personal development.

Healing Activity: Values and Boundaries Worksheet

1. List your top 5 personal values (e.g., honesty, respect, independence).
2. For each value, write down a specific boundary that would protect this value in a relationship.
3. Reflect on your current or past relationships. How well did/do they align with these values and boundaries?
4. Write a commitment to yourself about how you'll uphold these boundaries in future relationships.

Understanding Attachment Styles in Relationships

Our early experiences with caregivers shape our attachment styles, which in turn influence our adult relationships. Understanding your attachment style can provide valuable insights into your relationship patterns:

1. Secure Attachment: These individuals are comfortable with intimacy and independence. They can trust others and be trusted, and they have a positive view of themselves and their partners.

2. Anxious Attachment: People with this style often worry about their partner's availability and love. They may seek excessive reassurance and fear abandonment.

3. Avoidant Attachment: These individuals value independence highly and may be uncomfortable with close emotional connections. They might withdraw when things get too intimate.

4. Disorganized Attachment: This style combines anxious and avoidant behaviors. It often stems from traumatic experiences and can lead to chaotic relationship patterns.

Recognizing your attachment style doesn't mean you're locked into it. With self-awareness and effort, it's possible to develop a more secure attachment style over time.

Strategies for developing secure attachment:

1. Practice self-awareness and mindfulness
2. Communicate openly and honestly with partners
3. Work on building self-esteem and self-worth
4. Seek therapy to address underlying issues
5. Choose partners who are emotionally available and consistent

Remember, understanding your attachment style is a tool for growth, not a label that defines you. With patience and work, you can develop healthier relationship patterns and a more secure sense of self.

As we close this chapter, remember that every relationship, whether it lasts or not, offers an opportunity for growth and self-discovery. Your past does not dictate your future, but understanding it can help you make more conscious choices moving forward. Embrace your journey, with all its complexities, as each experience brings you closer to understanding yourself and what you truly need and deserve in love and life.

Chapter 4
Ties That Bind and Break

"Healing is not just mending the broken parts; it's creating a new whole."

After dating for nine years, my journey with my partner took a new turn when he proposed on my 29th birthday. It was a moment filled with conflicting emotions—joy at the prospect of building a life together, tinged with an undercurrent of anxiety about the enormity of this commitment.

Although I had never been the type of woman to dream about a fairytale wedding, I had always envisioned a destination wedding—something intimate and personal, with the backdrop of an exotic location. But that dream never came to fruition, and in hindsight, it was probably for the best. Maybe it was God's way of saving us the money, knowing our marriage wouldn't last. On New Year's Eve of that same year, we made our way to City Hall to get married, accompanied by our 5-year-old son. The choice of City Hall over a traditional ceremony was driven by financial constraints and the pressing need for me to be added to his medical plan quickly.

As we stood before the officiant, exchanging vows in the stark, administrative setting of City Hall, I couldn't shake the feeling that something was off. This wasn't the destination wedding I had once dreamed of, but I told myself it didn't matter. After all, we were already living like we were married. What difference could a piece of paper really make?

In my mind, marriage was just that—a piece of paper, a formality that wouldn't change the dynamics of our relationship. My attitude was, "If it ain't broke, don't fix it." We had a rhythm that worked for us, and I didn't see why a legal document should alter that. But my partner wanted to settle down and start a family officially, so we went ahead with it. Little did I know how profoundly this shift in our legal status would affect our relationship.

The first year of our marriage was a crucible, testing the very foundations of our relationship. I struggled immensely with my new role as a wife, finding the reality of marriage far different from the dating life we had enjoyed for almost a decade. There were unspoken expectations and pressures that neither of us had anticipated, creating a tension that seemed to permeate every aspect of our lives.

My wusband's expectations of what a wife should be made me feel trapped and inadequate. I constantly felt like I was failing to meet his standards, which eroded my self-esteem and sense of self-worth. A wife should be a partner, not an idealized figure of perfection. Marriage should be about mutual support and growth, not rigid roles and unrealistic expectations.

To cope with this overwhelming sense of losing myself, I turned to excessive shopping. What started as a way to fill the void and escape the pressures at home soon spiraled into an addiction. The momentary high of each purchase provided a fleeting sense of control, a temporary escape from the suffocating reality of my married life. But this coping mechanism came with its own set of problems. My habit spiraled out of control to the point where I even opened credit cards in my wusband's name without his knowledge to support my shopping binges, a decision that would later come back to haunt me with devastating consequences.

Our once easygoing relationship became tense and complicated. Small disagreements about finances and typical couple issues escalated into major arguments. The man who had once been my safe haven, my source of comfort and understanding, now seemed distant and unapproachable. My wusband would sometimes emotionally withdraw, giving me the silent treatment over matters that seemed trivial to me. His silence became its own form of emotional abuse, making me feel isolated and unimportant.

This emotional unavailability mirrored the unresolved issues I had with my father, triggering deep-seated fears of abandonment and unworthiness. I found myself trapped in a cycle of seeking validation from someone who could not provide it, replaying the painful dynamics of my childhood in my adult relationship. Less than a year after getting married, I made a terrible mistake by having a romantic affair. However, as things became more difficult at home, I found myself having more romantic affairs. These were misguided attempts to fill the emotional void I felt, desperate efforts to escape the pain and dissatisfaction in my marriage by finding temporary comfort in the arms of others. Each affair left me feeling guilty and ashamed, but also alive in a way I hadn't in a long time, creating a confusing mix of emotions that I struggled to reconcile.

In 2014, my estranged father died in his sleep. We hadn't spoken in over six months, and his passing brought a tidal wave of unresolved emotions — grief, anger, regret, and a profound sense of loss for the relationship we never truly had. My wusband and I had a disagreement the same week as the funeral, and we did not speak the entire time. This silence, this emotional abandonment during one of the most vulnerable periods of my life, made me feel incredibly alone and desperate to cling to my unhappy marriage. I believed my wusband was the only person who would be there for me since I no longer had surviving parents and no siblings. This belief, born out of fear and grief, only served to deepen my dependence on a relationship that was already fraught with problems.

Growing up, I witnessed many dysfunctional marriages marked by emotional absence, abuse, and conflict. This shaped my perception of relationships, making it difficult for me to recognize healthy dynamics and set boundaries. It's taken me years to unlearn those patterns and strive for a healthier understanding of what a relationship should be.

My reasons for seeking romantic affairs were complex and rooted in deep-seated issues. I felt neglected and unappreciated by my wusband, and the attention I received from others made me feel wanted and desirable. Each affair was a temporary fix, a way to numb the pain and boost my fragile self-esteem. I convinced myself that these encounters were justified, that I deserved to feel loved and desired, even if only for a fleeting moment.

But in reality, each affair was a betrayal of myself. I was cheating on more than just my wusband; I was cheating on my own values, my own sense of integrity, and my own potential for genuine happiness. Instead of addressing the root causes of my unhappiness, I was running away from them, creating a cycle of guilt and self-loathing that only deepened the emotional chasm I was trying to fill.

The turning point in my life came when my wusband accidentally discovered a sex video of me with another man on our son's phone. I had set up our son's phone using my Google account, and the video, meant to remain private, had synced to his device. My wusband, trying to free up space on our son's phone by deleting unnecessary content, stumbled across the video while I was napping.

I'll never forget the look in his eyes when he woke me up, holding the phone in his hand. I had barely opened my eyes when he began yelling, his voice like thunder. In an instant, he jumped on me, pinning me down. The rage in his face was something I'd never seen before, and all I could do was scream. My heart raced as fear gripped me. My mind spun in a whirlwind of regret, shame, and confusion. I wanted to disappear, to rewind time and erase everything that had led to this moment.

As he hurled accusations at me, my mind kept playing stories of my failures on repeat: How could I have done this? How could I hurt him so deeply? I had known all along that my actions were wrong, yet in this moment, it was more than guilt—it was pure self-loathing. I told myself I deserved this, that I was a horrible person, unworthy of love or forgiveness. I had ruined everything.

His words pierced me, each accusation leaving an indelible mark. Fear gripped me as I wondered what would happen next. I couldn't tell if he would hit me, leave me, or drag our son into the fight. The shame was overwhelming, making it hard to breathe. I felt like I had lost every ounce of dignity and control, and as he stood over me with the phone in his hand, it felt like my entire world was collapsing.

I kept telling myself I was broken, damaged beyond repair. Regret consumed me, along with the unbearable weight of everything I had destroyed. My marriage, my integrity, my future — gone. All I could do was lay there, as he yelled and raged, feeling like my mistakes had erased any possibility of redemption.

The discovery was a bombshell that detonated all the underlying issues we had been struggling with. In the aftermath, we decided to give our marriage another chance. We attended counseling and made a sincere effort to rebuild the trust that had been shattered. We spent countless hours talking through our issues, trying to find a path forward. For a while, it seemed like we might be able to salvage what was left of our marriage.

However, the discovery of the video left a scar that refused to heal. My wusband's suspicion grew, and despite my attempts to reassure him, he began to assume I was hiding another romantic relationship. His mistrust became a constant shadow over our lives, tainting even the smallest interactions. Every text message, every phone call, and every late return home was scrutinized. I could feel the weight of his doubts pressing down on me, and it was suffocating.

One night, during a particularly intense argument, the tension reached a breaking point. We were shouting, both of us lost in our anger and pain. My wusband accused me of lying, of deceiving him yet again. In a fit of rage, he pushed his forearm into my neck, pinning me against the wall. It was the first time he had ever laid a hand on me.

The assault and the reason that led to it also made me realize how crucial it is to prioritize not just physical safety but emotional safety as well. For anyone in a similar situation, I advise seeking help immediately if emotional abuse escalates to physical violence. It's essential to recognize that abuse, in any form, is unacceptable, and everyone deserves better.

In that moment, I realized just how far we had fallen. The man who had once been my confidant and partner had become someone I barely recognized, and I had contributed to this toxic environment with my own actions. The physical assault was a stark reminder of how destructive our relationship had become. It was a wake-up call that forced me to confront the reality of our situation.

I made the decision that he and I needed a break so that he could deal with the anger from my betrayals and stop placing the responsibility to heal him on myself. The more he threw my indiscretions in my face, the more guilt I felt for my actions, and the more anger I felt for the way he was making me feel.

That night, I knew that something had to change. We couldn't continue down this path of mutual destruction. For the first time in our marriage, I decided to stand up for myself. This decision marked the beginning of a new chapter, one where I would strive to find myself, self-respect, and what happiness truly meant for me.

Reflection Questions

1. Practice Radical Honesty: Start with being honest with yourself about your feelings, needs, and actions. Extend this honesty to your relationships, even when it's difficult.
2. Focus on Self-Care: Ensure your emotional well-being remains a priority, even in family dynamics.
3. Set Firm Boundaries: Clearly communicate what behaviors you will and will not tolerate.

4. Acknowledge Past Wounds: Recognize how past family trauma affects current relationships and take steps toward healing.

5. Prioritize Communication: Healthy relationships are built on open, honest communication — practice this in all relationships.

6. Allow Time for Growth: Relationships evolve over time — give space for healing and growth.

Tips for Healing

1. Practice Radical Honesty: Start with being honest with yourself about your feelings, needs, and actions. Extend this honesty to your relationships, even when it's difficult.

2. Seek Individual Therapy: Work through your personal issues and traumas with a professional who can provide tools for healing and growth.

3. Set Clear Boundaries: Identify what you will and won't accept in a relationship. Communicate these boundaries clearly and enforce them consistently.

4. Focus on Self-Care: Prioritize activities that nurture your physical, emotional, and mental well-being. Remember that you can't pour from an empty cup.

5. Learn from the Past: Reflect on your experiences and identify the lessons they've taught you. Use this knowledge to make more informed choices in the future.

Healing Activity: Letter to Your Future Self

Write a letter to your future self, five years from now. In this letter:

1. Describe the person you hope to become and the relationships you want to have.
2. List three specific actions you commit to taking to work towards this vision.
3. Include words of encouragement and compassion for the journey ahead.
4. Seal the letter and set a reminder to open it in five years.

This exercise helps you articulate your hopes and goals, and provides a touchstone for your personal growth journey.

Understanding Infidelity: A Complex Issue

Infidelity is often a symptom of deeper issues within a relationship or within oneself. While it's never justified, understanding the underlying factors can help in the healing process:

1. Emotional Disconnection: Often, affairs are a misguided attempt to fill an emotional void in the primary relationship.

2. Unresolved Personal Issues: Sometimes, infidelity is more about the individual's own unresolved traumas or self-esteem issues than about the relationship itself.

3. Poor Boundaries: Lack of clear boundaries in relationships can create situations where infidelity becomes more likely.

4. Unmet Needs: When significant needs (emotional, physical, or psychological) are consistently unmet in a relationship, some individuals may look outside the relationship to fulfill these needs.

5. Conflict Avoidance: For some, affairs are a way to avoid dealing with problems in the primary relationship.

6.   Desire for Novelty: Sometimes, the excitement of a new relationship can be alluring, especially in long-term partnerships that have become routine.

Healing from infidelity, whether you're the one who was unfaithful or the one who was betrayed, is a complex process that often requires professional help. It involves:

- Acknowledging the pain caused and taking responsibility for actions
- Exploring the root causes of the infidelity
- Rebuilding trust through consistent, honest behavior
- Improving communication within the relationship
- Working on individual issues that may have contributed to the situation
- Making a committed decision about the future of the relationship

Remember, healing is possible, but it requires dedication, honesty, and often, professional guidance. Whether the relationship continues or not, the goal is to learn from the experience and grow as individuals. As we conclude this chapter, remember that your past actions do not define your future. Every experience, even the painful ones, offers an opportunity for growth and self-discovery. The journey to healing and healthy relationships starts with being honest with yourself, taking responsibility for your actions, and committing to personal growth. You have the power to write the next chapter of your story, one that's filled with self-love, respect, and authentic connections.

Chapter 5
At the Edge

" Healing is about accepting the cracks and discovering the light that shines through. "

The decision to separate while still living together was, in hindsight, a recipe for disaster. Our home, once a sanctuary of love and shared dreams, had transformed into a battlefield of unspoken words and simmering resentment.

Every corner held memories of happier times, now tainted by the reality of our failing marriage. I didn't want to be with him romantically anymore, but I also wasn't ready to face life as a single woman. This limbo state, this in-between existence, was slowly poisoning my mind, eroding my sense of self and purpose.

As days blurred into weeks, I found myself sinking deeper into a pit of despair. The weight of my perceived failures — as a wife, a mother, a person — pressed down on me, making even the simplest tasks feel insurmountable. Each morning, I'd stare at the ceiling, willing myself to find the strength to face another day. The thought of getting out of bed, of putting on a brave face for the world, was exhausting. But I did it, day after day, forcing smiles that never reached my eyes, pretending I was okay when I was anything but. As time wore on, I found myself turning to wine more frequently, using it as a crutch to get through the evenings.

What started as an occasional glass turned into a nightly ritual. I'd come home from work, pour a glass — then another — and sit with it, hoping it would dull the emotional noise in my mind. But even that wasn't enough to calm the constant racing thoughts. I began taking anything I could find that would make me drowsy, mixing it with the wine to numb myself into sleep. It was the only way I knew to shut down the swirling chaos inside me, at least for a few hours.

At night, when the house fell quiet and I was left alone with my thoughts, the true extent of my pain revealed itself in my dreams. I found myself, night after night, hanging off the edge of a steep cliff, my fingers barely grasping the rocky ledge. The symbolism wasn't lost on me — I was quite literally at the edge, both in my dreams and in my waking life. What made these dreams even more unsettling was the presence of another "me." This other self was at the top of the cliff, desperately trying to pull me to safety. It was as if my psyche had split into two — the part of me that wanted to let go, to end the pain, and the part that was fighting to survive, to hold on despite the struggle. This internal tug-of-war was exhausting, leaving me drained and disoriented upon waking.

The intensity of these dreams was overwhelming. I could feel the strain in my arms, the panic rising in my chest, the wind whipping around me as I dangled over the abyss. It was a visceral representation of the internal battle I was fighting — the tug-of-war between my will to live and the exhaustion of constant emotional pain. Each time I woke from these dreams, I found myself drenched in a cold sweat, my heart racing as if I had actually been in physical danger. The fear and despair that permeated the dream lingered long after I opened my eyes, coloring my waking hours with a sense of dread and hopelessness.

Work became both a refuge and a battlefield. On one hand, it provided a temporary escape from the tension at home. On the other, it was becoming increasingly difficult to maintain the facade of normalcy. I was constantly on the verge of burnout, struggling to concentrate on tasks that once came easily to me. My colleagues saw a composed, functioning individual, but beneath the surface, I was barely treading water, expending enormous energy just to keep up appearances.

At home, the situation was even more unbearable. Every interaction with my wusband was fraught with tension and unresolved issues. Conversations that once flowed easily now felt like navigating a minefield. We both tried, for the sake of our son, to maintain some semblance of normalcy. But children are perceptive, and our son, innocent and unaware of the complexities of adult relationships, became the unwitting witness to our silent battles.

He would often ask questions that broke my heart — "Why don't you and dad laugh anymore?" or "Why is dad sleeping on the couch?" I struggled to find answers that wouldn't burden him with adult concerns, all while grappling with my own guilt for exposing him to such a toxic environment. The weight of potentially damaging my child's emotional well-being added another layer to my already overwhelming sense of failure.

The weight of my family issues compounded my sense of isolation. Without living parents or siblings to turn to, I felt completely alone in my struggle. The void left by my mother's death years ago felt more pronounced than ever. I longed for her guidance, her comforting presence — anything to anchor me in this storm of emotions. This lack of a support system made my emotional spiral feel even more inescapable, as if I was falling with no one to catch me.

As the days wore on, the darkness within me grew. The pain, the loneliness, the feeling of utter failure — it all became too much to bear. Thoughts of ending it all, once fleeting and easily dismissed, now took root in my mind. They whispered seductively, promising an end to the pain, a final escape from the mess I'd made of my life. These thoughts were terrifying, but also strangely comforting, offering a way out of the emotional turmoil that had become my daily existence.

It was on a day that felt particularly hopeless that I made the decision. I remember feeling a strange sense of calm as I gathered the pills. In my distorted state of mind, I truly believed that everyone would be better off without me. My son would have a father who could provide stability, unburdened by a mother who couldn't seem to get her life together. My wusband would be free to find happiness with someone else — someone who could be the wife he deserved. The twisted logic of depression had convinced me that my absence would be a gift to those I loved, freeing them from the burden I believed myself to be.

I sent a final text to my wusband: *"Thanks for not throwing away my pills."* It was a cryptic message, a silent plea for acknowledgment of my pain. Part of me hoped he would understand, that he would rush home and stop me. Another part—the part that was tired of fighting—hoped he wouldn't. This internal conflict, this simultaneous desire to be saved and to disappear, epitomized the complex, contradictory nature of suicidal thoughts.

The next thing I remember is waking up in the hospital. The harsh fluorescent lights burned my eyes, and the cacophony of beeping machines and distant voices felt overwhelming. As my vision cleared, I saw my aunt sitting beside me, her face a mixture of worry and relief. Across the room stood my wusband, his expression a complex blend of anger, confusion, and fear.

As I lay there, grappling with the reality of what I had done and the fact that I was still alive, I felt a whirlpool of conflicting emotions. I was alive, but I didn't want to be. There was a dull ache in my chest, a void that seemed impossible to fill. I felt like a failure—I couldn't even succeed at ending my own life. The shame of my actions weighed heavily on me, yet I couldn't deny the small flicker of relief that being here, being alive, brought.

The guilt hit me in waves as I thought about my son. My beautiful, innocent 11-year-old boy, who nearly lost his mother to the demons she couldn't fight. The image of his face filled my mind, and I was overwhelmed by the realization of what I had almost done. How could I have considered leaving him motherless, subjecting him to the same pain I had experienced when I lost my own mother?

This guilt was crushing, but it also became a lifeline — a reason to fight against the darkness that had nearly consumed me. As I lay in that sterile hospital room, surrounded by the tangible evidence of my darkest moment, I realized that this was not just my battle — it was his too. He deserved better. He deserved a mother who could fight through the darkness and find the strength to keep going. This realization became the first fragile thread of hope, a reason to try to make sense of the chaos and find a way forward. The road ahead was long and daunting. I knew that surviving this attempt was just the beginning. There would be therapy, medications, difficult conversations, and a lot of hard work ahead. But as I looked at my aunt's tearful smile and felt the weight of my wusband's conflicted gaze, I made a silent promise to my son and to myself. I would fight. I would heal. I would find a way to silence the demons that had brought me to this edge.

It wouldn't be easy. There would be days when the darkness would feel overwhelming, when the pull of despair would be strong. But I had been given a second chance, and I owed it to my son, to myself, to make the most of it. One day at a time, one small step at a time, I would find my way back to life, back to hope, back to the mother and person I knew I could be.

This was my turning point — my rock bottom, but also my beginning. The journey of healing starts here, in this hospital room, with the realization that my life has value, that I am loved, and that there is hope, even in the darkest of times. It's a journey I'm now committed to, not just for myself, but for my son, for my family, and for anyone else who might be standing at the edge, wondering if they should let go. To them, I say: hold on. There is light ahead, even if you can't see it yet. Your story isn't over. Mine isn't either. We're just beginning a new chapter.

Reflection Questions

1. Have you ever felt like you were at a breaking point? What helped you get through it?

2. How do you recognize when your mental health is deteriorating? What are your personal warning signs?

3. How has the concept of surrender helped you in your healing journey?

4. How do you balance your own mental health needs with your responsibilities to others, especially children?

5. What does resilience mean to you? How have you seen resilience in your own life or in others?

Tips for Healing

1. Lean Into Vulnerability: Allow yourself to feel your emotions, as painful as they might be, without judgment.

2. Find Strength in Surrender: Sometimes, the greatest strength comes from accepting where you are without needing to "fix" everything immediately.

3. Build a Support Network: Identify trusted friends or family members you can turn to when you're struggling. Sometimes, just knowing you're not alone can make a big difference.

4. Practice Mindful Reflection: Take time to reflect on your journey and the steps you've taken, both good and bad.

5. Establish a Routine: Creating structure in your day can provide a sense of normalcy and purpose, even when everything else feels chaotic.

6. Celebrate Small Victories: Every step forward, no matter how small, is a sign of growth.

Healing Activity: Creating a Hope Box

A Hope Box is a tangible reminder of reasons to live and things that bring you joy. To create one:

1. Find a box or container that feels special to you.

2. Fill it with items that make you feel positive or remind you of happy times. These could include:
   - Photos of loved ones or happy memories
   - Letters or cards from friends and family
   - Small objects that have positive associations
   - A list of your accomplishments or things you're proud of
   - Inspiring quotes or affirmations

3. Add items that engage your senses, like a favorite tea bag or a small bottle of essential oil.

4. Include a list of coping strategies that have worked for you in the past.

5. Add contact information for your support network and crisis helplines.

Keep your Hope Box easily accessible and turn to it when you're feeling low or overwhelmed.

Understanding Suicidal Ideation A Cry for Help

Suicidal thoughts, also known as suicidal ideation, are complex and often misunderstood. They're not a sign of weakness, but rather an indication of overwhelming pain and a desperate desire for that pain to end. Understanding suicidal ideation can help both those experiencing it and those supporting loved ones:

1. It's More Common Than You Think: Many people have fleeting thoughts of suicide at some point in their lives, especially during times of extreme stress or loss.

2. It Exists on a Spectrum: Suicidal ideation can range from fleeting thoughts to detailed plans. All levels should be taken seriously.

3. It's Often Linked to Mental Health Conditions: Depression, anxiety, PTSD, and other mental health issues can increase the risk of suicidal thoughts.

4. It's Not Always Visible: Many people experiencing suicidal thoughts hide their pain from others, sometimes out of shame or fear of being a burden.

5. It's Treatable: With proper support and treatment, many people overcome suicidal thoughts and go on to live fulfilling lives.

6. It's Not Selfish: People considering suicide often believe (incorrectly) that others would be better off without them.

7. Talking About It Helps: Contrary to popular belief, asking someone if they're having suicidal thoughts doesn't increase the risk - it often provides relief and opens the door for help.

If you or someone you know is experiencing suicidal thoughts:

- Reach out for help immediately. Call a suicide prevention hotline or seek emergency medical care.

- Remember that these feelings are temporary, even if they don't feel that way right now.

- Connect with others. Isolation can worsen suicidal thoughts.

- Remove access to lethal means, such as firearms or large quantities of medication.
- Engage in safety planning with a mental health professional.

Remember, seeking help is a sign of strength, not weakness. Recovery is possible, and you deserve support in finding your way back to hope and life.

As we close this chapter, remember that your darkest moment doesn't define you - it's a part of your story, but not the end of it. Every day you choose to keep going is an act of courage and hope. You are stronger than you know, and your life has value beyond what you can see right now. The journey of healing may be long and challenging, but it's also filled with opportunities for growth, self-discovery, and renewed purpose. You are not alone on this journey, and there is always hope, even in the darkest of times.

Chapter 6
The Road to Recovery

"Healing is a journey, not a destination. Each day is a step forward, no matter how small."

After my suicide attempt, I was held in the hospital for eight slow days. Those eight days were a blur of constant monitoring, forced conversations with doctors, and an overwhelming sense of isolation. The sterile environment of the hospital, with its stark white walls and the constant beeping of machines, felt both like a sanctuary and a prison. I was safe from myself, yet trapped with the very thoughts and emotions that had brought me there.

In those first few days, I couldn't decide if I was relieved or resentful to be there. Part of me was grateful for the forced stillness — away from the chaos of my mind and the expectations of the outside world. But another part of me, the part that had wanted to give up entirely, felt betrayed by my own survival. The hospital, with its rigid schedule and clinical atmosphere, felt too clean, too detached from the storm inside me. I wasn't sure if I was grateful to be saved or simply angry that I had failed in my attempt.

Most of my days consisted of reading, coloring pictures, and eating, trying to pass the time. There was a numbness in those actions, as if I were simply going through the motions of life without actually living. It was easier to lose myself in the monotony than to confront the reality of what had brought me there. The monotony was occasionally broken by visits from healthcare professionals, their clipboards and concerned expressions a constant reminder of why I was there. Being kept under watch felt like a sentence, but it was a necessary one — a buffer between the darkness that had consumed me and the uncertain light of recovery.

But even as I followed the routine, I could feel the weight of my own thoughts pressing in on me. There was no escaping the internal dialogue, the relentless voice that reminded me of everything I had lost, everything I had broken. It was as if the quiet of the hospital amplified the noise in my head. I kept wondering how I had ended up there — what had gone so wrong that this sterile room had become my reality. And yet, a part of me understood that this was where I needed to be. Not because I wanted to be, but because there was no other choice.

During my stay, my aunt and closest friends came to visit me. Their presence was a bittersweet reminder of the life outside those sterile walls. I tried to make light of the situation by sarcastically greeting them with, "Welcome to my humble abode," hoping to ease the tension. While their visits provided brief moments of comfort and distraction, they also highlighted the gravity of my situation. It was difficult to see the concern and worry in their eyes, knowing I had caused them such pain. Their love was palpable, but so was their fear — fear of losing me, fear of saying the wrong thing, fear of not being able to help.

I could feel the weight of their worry, even when they didn't say much. There was an unspoken tension in every visit, a delicate balance between their desire to be there for me and the uncertainty of how to do that. And I hated it. I hated that I had put them in this position, that I had become the source of their pain. There was a deep shame in that, a shame I couldn't shake no matter how much they tried to hide their fear behind supportive smiles and kind words. I kept wondering what they must think of me now. How had I gone from being someone they could rely on to someone they needed to save?

Amid this challenging period, I was introduced to the Emotions Anonymous (EA) program when two members visited the behavioral health unit. Their visit was a turning point, offering a glimpse of hope and community support. One of the members even gifted me the Emotions Anonymous book, a gesture that touched me deeply. They encouraged me to attend the EA meetings after my discharge, planting a seed of possibility for a support system beyond the hospital walls.

Their visit felt different from the others. Maybe it was because, for the first time, I was talking to people who truly understood what I was going through. They didn't look at me with pity or fear. They looked at me with understanding, and that was something I hadn't realized I desperately needed. I had spent so long feeling like an outsider in my own life, disconnected from everyone around me, but in those few moments, I felt a flicker of belonging. It was small, barely enough to hold onto, but it was there. And in the midst of everything else, that flicker felt like hope.

I met with a psychiatrist and a social worker regularly during my stay. In one of my conversations with the social worker, I mentioned that I often wondered if I was bipolar. This information was relayed to the psychiatrist, who decided to treat me for bipolar disorder, prescribing a cocktail of medications, including Lithium, an antidepressant, and Trazodone, a sleep aid that didn't really help me sleep. The irony wasn't lost on me — being prescribed so many pills after a suicide attempt by overdosing. It seemed like a cruel joke, a reminder of how close I had come to ending it all.

But I understood the necessity. These medications were meant to be tools for stabilizing my mood, not potential weapons for self-harm. Still, the weight of the pill bottles in my hand each morning and evening was a sobering reminder of the fragility of my mental state.

There was a part of me that resisted the pills. Not because I didn't want to get better, but because taking them felt like an admission that something was wrong with me, something fundamentally broken. And maybe I wasn't ready to admit that yet. Swallowing those pills each day was like swallowing the reality of my situation, and some days, that reality was too hard to face. But I did it anyway, because deep down, I knew I needed help. And maybe, just maybe, this was the first step toward something better.

The release from the hospital came with a condition: I had to attend an intensive outpatient program, running Monday to Friday for seven hours a day for four weeks. This program focused on structured therapeutic sessions, which were demanding but necessary. Following the completion of this program, I transitioned to the Partial Hospitalization Program, where I was only required to attend half days. This gradual step-down approach was designed to ease the transition back into daily life while still providing substantial support.

On the first day of the outpatient program, I felt a mix of apprehension and reluctant hope. As I sat in the room, surrounded by others who were clearly battling their own demons, a sense of camaraderie mixed with deep-seated fear. We were all there for different reasons, but our paths had led us to the same place. The initial sessions involved a lot of talking—sharing our stories, our pain, and our fears. It was uncomfortable and raw, but it was also the first time I began to make sense of my emotions and the feelings that had led to my attempt.

The first few days were the hardest. The program was structured and intense, with sessions starting early in the morning and ending late in the afternoon. There was something cathartic about hearing others' stories and realizing I wasn't alone in my suffering. But it was also exhausting, emotionally and physically. Each day felt like peeling back another layer of pain, exposing raw nerves and long-buried emotions.

My psychiatrist formally diagnosed me with bipolar disorder during this time, and immediately prescribed Lithium and an anti-depressant. This diagnosis was not at all that shocking, especially since I told the Social Worker that I often wondered if I had bipolar. I had always felt like my emotions were on a rollercoaster — extreme highs followed by devastating lows. The diagnosis explained so much about my life, from my impulsive decisions to the complexities of my misery.

It was both a relief and a new burden to bear, a label that offered understanding but also carried its own weight of stigma and uncertainty. Putting a name to what I had been experiencing didn't make it any easier to accept. In fact, it forced me to confront the fact that my struggles weren't just fleeting moments — they were part of a larger battle I would have to face for the rest of my life.

The people I met in the program were incredible. Each person had a unique story, and their strength inspired me. Despite their own battles, they were there to fight, to find a way to live another day. Their courage gave me hope, showing me that recovery was possible, even when it felt impossible. I admired them deeply, but part of me wondered if I had the same strength they did. They seemed so sure of their need to recover, while I still felt like I was floating in a sea of uncertainty. But I kept showing up, telling myself that maybe just being there was enough for now.

However, the program also brought up many of my own unresolved mental health issues. I had to confront my fears, my guilt, and my pain head-on. It was exhausting, both mentally and emotionally. There were days when I wanted to quit, to give up, and let the darkness consume me. But I kept going, driven by a newfound determination to heal and find a way to live a fulfilling life. Some days, I wasn't sure where that determination came from, but I clung to it. I realized that healing wasn't about grand gestures or sudden breakthroughs. It was about the small, everyday choices to keep moving forward, even when it felt impossible.

As I continued my journey through the outpatient program, I learned valuable coping mechanisms and strategies to manage my bipolar disorder. It was a slow process, but I was discovering new things about myself each day. I began to understand my triggers, to recognize the early signs of manic or depressive episodes, and to develop strategies for managing my symptoms.

One of the most significant breakthroughs came during a group therapy session focused on forgiveness. We were discussing the importance of forgiveness — not just forgiving others but also forgiving ourselves. This concept resonated deeply with me. I had been carrying so much guilt and shame for my past actions, and it was eating away at my ability to heal. The idea that I could forgive myself, that I deserved forgiveness, was both terrifying and liberating.

It was also during this time that I realized my struggles with mental health began long before my recent crisis. When I was twenty-three, a therapist diagnosed me with depression. This diagnosis came shortly before I became pregnant with my son. At the time, I was in denial and afraid of the stigma attached to mental illness. I refused to accept the diagnosis, telling her that I wasn't depressed, just lazy — which was why I stayed in bed daily. Now, with the perspective of time and therapy, I saw how deeply I had been in denial, avoiding the truth about my mental health.

Returning home to my wusband and son after the attempt was one of the most challenging parts of my recovery. The house, which once felt like a safe haven, now felt toxic and suffocating. My wusband and I were still not on good terms; I always felt that my attempt had scared him to the point that he was afraid of coming home to find me no longer alive, with our son there to witness it. The trust had been shattered, and the air was thick with tension. My son, who was too young to fully understand, sensed the unease, and it broke my heart to see him caught in the middle.

When I returned home, I was hoping for compassion and understanding more than anything. But the reality was complicated. The dynamics of our relationship had shifted, and we were all struggling to find our footing in this new reality. It's crucial for loved ones to create a non-judgmental and supportive environment for someone recovering from a suicide attempt. They should express their love and concern without pressuring the person to explain their actions immediately. Gentle reassurance, patience, and a willingness to listen can make a significant difference in how a person feels after such a traumatic event.

s

Despite the toxicity of my home environment, I was terrified of moving out on my own. The thought of being alone, especially without the constant presence of my son, was daunting. However, I eventually realized that I had no choice and had to step into this new chapter of uncertainty.

We agreed that our son would live primarily with his dad. I didn't feel mentally capable of being a good mother at the time, and I believed a boy needs a father to show him how to be a man. Since I wasn't and never would be a man, I didn't argue with this decision. The choice was heartbreaking but necessary. Although comments from family and friends about my decision weighed heavily on me, I knew my son needed stability, and at that moment, his father could provide it better than I could.

My mental state after the attempt was fragile. I was grappling with a whirlwind of emotions — guilt, shame, fear, and a lingering sense of hopelessness. Each day felt like a battle to keep myself together, to maintain some semblance of normalcy for the sake of my son. There were moments when the weight of my despair felt unbearable, and I struggled to find the motivation to continue. The fear of another breakdown loomed over me, and I constantly worried about the impact of my instability on my family. Every interaction with my wusband was strained, filled with unspoken anxieties and unresolved pain. The house felt like a minefield, and I was constantly on edge, fearing the next emotional explosion. My son's innocence and his need for a stable, loving environment were the only things that kept me fighting to hold on.

After my attempt, everything felt different. It was like my world had shifted, and I couldn't find my footing. I felt disconnected from everyone around me, even those who tried to be supportive. Every interaction was layered with anxiety and mistrust. It was like walking through a dense fog, where everything and everyone seemed distant and unreachable. This isn't unusual for many who have been suicidal; the intense emotions and thoughts that led to the attempt often stick around, making it incredibly hard to reconnect with life and the people in it.

The familiar faces of friends and family now seemed strange, and I couldn't shake the feeling that they saw me differently too. I was hyper-aware of their reactions, convinced they viewed me with a mix of pity and fear. This only deepened my sense of isolation and unworthiness.

Inside my mind, the relentless inner critic was louder than ever, magnifying every mistake and perceived shortcoming. The shame gnawed at me constantly, reminding me of my failures as a mother, a wife, and a person. The nights were the worst; the silence amplified my racing thoughts and fears. Sleep was elusive, and when it did come, it was often interrupted by nightmares that left me more exhausted than before.

My distorted view of reality made it hard to see any possibility of improvement. The despair clouded my judgment and skewed my perception of myself and others. I felt trapped in a never-ending cycle of hopelessness, struggling to find a way to reconnect with a world that seemed so distant and unwelcoming.

The confusion of my emotions created a fog that I struggled to navigate. One moment I felt a flicker of hope, thinking that maybe things could get better. The next I was plunged back into darkness, convinced that nothing would ever improve. This emotional volatility made it difficult to trust myself or my decisions. I often second-guessed every action, wondering if it would be the one to trigger another crisis. Despite the pain and confusion, I held on to the small moments of joy with my son. His laughter was a brief respite from the chaos, a reminder of the love that still existed amidst the turmoil. These moments, though fleeting, were my lifeline, small beacons of light in the darkness that surrounded me.

Returning to a toxic home environment after my attempt underscored the need for a supportive and understanding space. I would encourage families and friends of suicide attempt survivors to create an environment that is nurturing, empathetic, and free of judgment. It's essential to provide a safe space where the person feels loved and supported without the pressure to immediately explain or justify their actions.

Create a supportive environment by showing unconditional love and acceptance, providing a sense of security, and being a reliable source of comfort and strength during a profoundly challenging time. Offer a listening ear without jumping to conclusions or giving unsolicited advice. It means being patient and allowing the person to share their feelings at their own pace. Small gestures of kindness and reassurance can go a long way towards making someone feel valued and understood. Avoiding blame or criticism is crucial, as these can push the person further into isolation and despair.

Encouraging professional help and being there to support them through their treatment process is also vital. This can include helping them keep appointments, offering to drive them, or simply checking in on their progress. Creating a routine that includes regular check-ins and positive activities can help rebuild a sense of normalcy and stability.

Families and friends should also educate themselves about mental health and the specific challenges faced by those who have attempted suicide. Understanding the underlying issues can foster empathy and enable more effective support. It's important to recognize that healing is a gradual process, and there will be ups and downs. Being consistent in offering love, support, and understanding can make a significant difference in the recovery journey.

As I continue on this path of recovery, I'm learning that healing is not linear. There are good days and bad days, steps forward and steps back. But with each passing day, I'm growing stronger, more resilient, and more committed to my own well-being and that of my son. This journey has taught me the true meaning of self-love, the importance of seeking help, and the power of taking it one day at a time. I'm not where I want to be yet, but I'm not where I was either. And that, in itself, is progress worth celebrating.

Reflection Questions

1. How has your understanding of mental health changed over time? Have you ever experienced a shift in perspective about your own mental health?

2. How do you process feelings of anger or resentment during your healing journey?

3. Have you ever had to confront a part of yourself or your past that you were in denial about? How did you navigate that process?

4. What small victories have you celebrated in your own journey of growth or healing?

5. How do you balance self-care and caring for others,

6. especially during challenging times?

Tips for Healing

1. Establish a Routine: Create daily habits that bring you peace and structure. This could include a morning meditation, an evening walk, or a bedtime reading ritual.

2. Practice Mindfulness: Engage in activities like yoga or meditation to connect with your body and mind. These practices can help ground you in the present moment.

3. Set Small, Achievable Goals: Focus on small, daily objectives. Accomplishing these can boost your confidence and provide a sense of progress.

4. Journaling: Keep a journal to track your thoughts, feelings, and progress. This can be a powerful tool for self-reflection and recognizing patterns in your mood and behavior.

5. Seek Professional Help: Don't hesitate to reach out for therapy or counseling during difficult moments.

Healing Activity
Gratitude and Progress Journal

Start a daily journaling practice with two main components:

1. Gratitude: Each day, write down three things you're grateful for. They can be big or small.

2. Progress: Note one thing you did that day that represents progress, no matter how small. It could be getting out of bed, calling a friend, or attending a therapy session.

At the end of each week, review your entries. Reflect on the positive aspects of your life and acknowledge the steps you've taken, no matter how small they might seem.

Understanding Bipolar Disorder Navigating the Highs and Lows

Bipolar disorder is a complex mental health condition characterized by significant mood swings that include emotional highs (mania or hypomania) and lows (depression). Understanding this condition is crucial for those diagnosed and their support systems:

1. Types of Bipolar Disorder:
   - Bipolar I: Characterized by manic episodes that last at least 7 days, or severe manic symptoms that require immediate hospital care. Depressive episodes also occur, typically lasting at least 2 weeks.
   - Bipolar II: Involves a pattern of depressive episodes and hypomanic episodes, but not the full-blown manic episodes typical of Bipolar I.
2. Symptoms of Manic Episodes:
   - Increased energy and activity
   - Euphoria or irritability
   - Racing thoughts and rapid speech
   - Decreased need for sleep
   - Impulsive or risky behavior

3. Symptoms of Depressive Episodes:
   - Persistent sadness or emptiness
   - Loss of interest in activities
   - Changes in appetite and sleep patterns
   - Fatigue and loss of energy
   - Feelings of worthlessness or guilt

4. Treatment Approaches:
   - Medication: Mood stabilizers, antipsychotics, and sometimes antidepressants
   - Psychotherapy: Cognitive Behavioral Therapy (CBT), Interpersonal and Social Rhythm Therapy (IPSRT)
   - Lifestyle changes: Regular sleep schedule, stress management, avoiding alcohol and drugs

5. Living with Bipolar Disorder:
   - Understand your triggers and warning signs
   - Stick to your treatment plan
   - Build a strong support network
   - Educate yourself and your loved ones about the condition
   - Practice stress-reduction techniques
   - Maintain a consistent sleep schedule
   - Avoid alcohol and recreational drugs

6. Supporting Someone with Bipolar Disorder:
    - Learn about the condition
    - Encourage them to stick to their treatment plan
    - Be patient and understanding, especially during mood episodes
    - Help them maintain a stable routine
    - Know the warning signs of manic or depressive episodes
    - Have a plan for manic or depressive crises

Remember, bipolar disorder is a manageable condition. With proper treatment and support, many people with bipolar disorder lead fulfilling, productive lives. The key is patience, persistence, and a commitment to ongoing care and self-management.

As we conclude this chapter on the road to recovery, it's important to recognize that healing is not a linear journey. There will be ups and downs, progress and setbacks. But each step, no matter how small, is a victory worth celebrating.

Recovery from a suicide attempt, managing bipolar disorder, or navigating any mental health challenge requires courage, resilience, and support. It's about learning to be gentle with yourself, to recognize your own strength, and to reach out for help when you need it.

Remember that you are not defined by your diagnosis or your past actions. You are a complex, valuable human being deserving of love, respect, and happiness. Your journey of recovery is uniquely yours, and it's okay if it doesn't look like anyone else's.

As you move forward, hold onto hope. Even in the darkest moments, remember that change is possible. You've already shown immense strength by surviving, by seeking help, by continuing to fight. That strength will carry you forward.

To those supporting loved ones on their recovery journey, your role is invaluable. Your patience, understanding, and unwavering support can make a world of difference. Remember to also take care of your own mental health in the process. Healing takes time, effort, and often professional help. But it is possible. Each day is an opportunity to take another step forward, to learn something new about yourself, to grow stronger and more resilient. You are not alone on this journey. There is help, there is hope, and there is a future worth fighting for.

As we move into the next chapter, carry with you the knowledge that you are stronger than you know, more resilient than you believe, and worthy of all the good things life has to offer. Your story isn't over; in many ways, it's just beginning

Chapter 7
New Beginnings

"Healing doesn't mean the damage never existed. It means the damage no longer controls our lives."

Filing for divorce was an act of bravery. It was me standing up for myself, acknowledging that I deserved more than a life of emotional neglect and pain. It was me choosing to prioritize my mental and emotional well-being over the comfort of what was known, even if it was harmful. This step marked a significant turning point in my life — a powerful affirmation that I was capable of making decisions that were in my best interest.

Closing this chapter allowed me to move forward unencumbered by the weight of a failing marriage. It freed me to fully embrace the healing and growth I had worked so hard to achieve. I felt empowered, knowing that I had the strength to make complex decisions and the resilience to see them through. This decision was a testament to my growth and a reminder of the inner strength I had discovered through my journey of self-discovery and healing. By filing for divorce, I not only ended a chapter of my life but also opened the door to new beginnings. It was a powerful step towards a future filled with possibility, hope, and a renewed sense of self.

Reflecting on this period of solitude during COVID, I realized how important it was to sit with my thoughts. For someone experiencing suicidal ideation, sitting with their thoughts can be a double-edged sword. It can be healthy if done in a supportive environment, where they feel safe and can process their emotions constructively. However, it's crucial to have a support system in place to ensure they are not overwhelmed by their thoughts. Encouraging them to seek professional help, join support groups, and engage in activities that promote mental well-being can make a significant difference. In this time of deep reflection, I also realized that solitude had given me the space I needed to really listen to myself — something I had avoided for so long. There was no one to distract me, no one to appease or perform for. It was just me, and in that solitude, I discovered that I was stronger than I thought.

The quiet allowed me to confront painful emotions and unresolved wounds that I had kept buried for years, and while it wasn't easy, it was necessary. It was in these moments of sitting with my thoughts that I began to understand that healing wasn't about erasing the damage or pretending it hadn't happened. It was about reclaiming my narrative and choosing to no longer be controlled by the pain.

To change a negative situation like COVID or divorce into a positive one, I would encourage anyone to focus on self-improvement and growth. Use the time to explore new hobbies, learn new skills, and engage in activities that bring you joy and fulfillment. Finding a purpose or setting small, achievable goals can help shift the focus from the negative aspects to positive progress. Celebrate your milestones, no matter how small, as a victory.

Volunteering or helping others, even in small ways, can provide a sense of purpose and community connection. Connecting with others through virtual meetups or learning communities can foster a sense of belonging and support. Engaging in mindfulness practices such as meditation or journaling can help process emotions and bring a sense of peace and clarity.

Additionally, taking time for self-care is crucial. Develop routines that prioritize your well-being, such as regular sleep patterns, healthy eating, and taking breaks to relax and recharge. Surround yourself with positivity, whether it's through inspirational podcasts, uplifting music, or spending time with loved ones who support and encourage you.

By focusing on these positive actions, you can transform a challenging situation into an opportunity for growth and self-discovery, emerging stronger and more resilient. This journey of healing and self-discovery is ongoing, and each day brings new opportunities for growth and understanding. Remember, healing is not about erasing the past, but about learning from it and using those lessons to create a brighter, more fulfilling future.

Reflection Questions

1. How have you reclaimed your personal power through moments of ending or new beginnings?

2. What steps have you taken to create a nurturing environment for yourself, both physically and emotionally?

3. How has your relationship with your past evolved as you've worked on healing?

4. What role has forgiveness - of others and yourself - played in your personal growth?

5. How do you honor both your healing process and the part of you that still carries pain

Tips for Healing

1. Create a Sanctuary: Design your living space to reflect the peace and positivity you want in your life.

2. Practice Mindfulness: Incorporate daily meditation or mindfulness exercises to stay grounded and present.

3. Own Your Power: Acknowledge your strength in making tough decisions, especially those that protect your emotional and mental health.

4. Seek Community: Find support groups or communities that align with your journey of growth and healing.

5. Embrace New Experiences: Challenge yourself to try new things that promote personal growth and self-discovery.

Healing Activity
Vision Board for Your New Chapter

Create a vision board that represents the new chapter of your life you're stepping into:

1. Gather magazines, printed photos, quotes, or any visual materials that resonate with you.

2. Choose a board or large piece of paper as your base.

3. Cut out images, words, or phrases that represent your goals, dreams, and the person you're becoming.

4. Arrange and glue these items on your board in a way that feels meaningful to you.

5. Place your vision board somewhere you'll see it daily as a reminder of your journey and aspirations.

This activity helps you visualize your future and keeps you focused on your goals for personal growth and healing.

Understanding the Power of Solitude in Healing

Solitude, when approached mindfully, can be a powerful tool for healing and self-discovery:

1. Self-Reflection: Solitude provides the space needed for deep self-reflection, allowing you to examine your thoughts, feelings, and behaviors without external distractions.

2. Emotional Processing: It gives you time to process complex emotions at your own pace, without the pressure of immediate responses or judgments from others.

3. Creativity and Problem-Solving: Solitude can boost creativity and improve problem-solving skills by

allowing your mind to wander and make new connections.

4. Stress Reduction: Time alone can help reduce stress and anxiety by providing a break from social pressures and expectations.

5. Self-Reliance: It fosters independence and self-reliance, helping you become more comfortable with yourself and your own company.

6. Clarity of Purpose: Solitude can help you clarify your goals, values, and what truly matters to you without the influence of others' opinions.

7. Resetting Relationships: Time alone can help you reassess your relationships and how they impact your life, leading to healthier connections.

8. Spiritual Growth: For many, solitude is essential for spiritual practices and growth, providing time for prayer, meditation, or connection with a higher power.

However, it's important to balance solitude with social connection. While time alone is valuable, humans are inherently social creatures who also need meaningful connections with others. The key is finding the right balance that supports your healing and growth.

If solitude becomes isolation or leads to increased negative thoughts, it's crucial to reach out for support. Remember, healing often involves a combination of self-reflection, professional help, and community support.

Remember that new beginnings are always possible. Every day offers an opportunity to rewrite your story, to choose growth over stagnation, and to move towards the life you envision for yourself. Your past has shaped you, but it does not define your future. Embrace the lessons, forgive the mistakes, and step boldly into the new chapter you're creating.

You have the strength within you to heal, to grow, and to create a life filled with purpose and joy. Trust in your journey, celebrate your progress, and keep moving forward, one day at a time.

Chapter 8
Reconnecting & Rediscovering

"Every step towards healing is a step towards rediscovering the essence of who you truly are."

As I continued to heal, I found myself on a path of reconnection - not just with others, but with the deepest parts of myself that I had long neglected or forgotten. This journey of rediscovery led me to explore avenues I had not considered before, pushing the boundaries of my understanding and opening myself to new experiences that would profoundly shape my healing process.

One day at a time, I found myself in a much better place mentally and emotionally. While I still had my bad days, I had built resilience and gathered the tools needed to get through them. One tool that was particularly effective was positive affirmations, which I posted throughout my home.

These affirmations provided encouragement from the moment I opened my eyes in the morning to the last moment before I closed them at night. In addition to the affirmations, I started putting up pictures of myself smiling—visual proof that life could be beautiful, even if some days were harder than others. On my bad days, those images and words were reminders that this, too, shall pass and that joy would always find its way back.

Despite this newfound resilience, there was still a part of me that ached. Healing wasn't linear, and I realized I had years of unresolved pain tucked away, pain I thought I had buried for good. Each day brought its challenges, but it also brought opportunities to peel back the layers of hurt, revealing the parts of me I had long shielded from view. It became clear that my healing journey was not just about recent events but about addressing the wounds from my past—those moments in life where I had been broken, fragmented, and forgotten.

This chapter of my life was about healing, not just from recent events, but also from the long-standing wounds that had shaped my journey. It was a time of confronting old pain, of facing the shadows I had long tried to outrun, and of finding the courage to embrace all parts of myself - even the parts that scared me.

Part of this healing journey involved making amends, both to my wusband and to myself. I knew that to move forward, I had to address the hurt and harm I had caused him. With a mixture of trepidation and determination, I decided to send an email, pouring out my heartfelt apology for the pain, disrespect, and betrayal he endured because of my actions. It was important for me to take responsibility and express my sincere regret for the way I had hurt him.

Crafting that email was one of the hardest things I've ever done. Each word felt heavy with the weight of our shared history, the pain we had caused each other, and the future we had lost. But as I wrote, I felt a sense of release, as if each admission of wrongdoing was loosening a knot inside me that I hadn't even realized was there.

I also needed to forgive myself, and this step was crucial in that process. To my relief, my wusband graciously accepted my apology. We eventually talked about it in person, and it was a deeply emotional conversation. He took accountability for his lack of emotional support and expressed his own regrets, apologizing for the ways he had contributed to our difficulties.

Hearing his acceptance and forgiveness was a significant step in my own journey toward self-forgiveness. It didn't erase the past, but it allowed us both to acknowledge our shared pain and the growth that had come from it. This conversation marked a turning point in our relationship, opening the door to a new kind of connection based on mutual understanding and respect.

Since then, we have created a new platonic and loving co-parenting relationship. Our bond, though transformed, remains strong through our shared love for our son. We have both moved on to new relationships, but we continue to support each other. The mutual respect and care we now share have fostered a healthier environment for our son, showing him that love and support can exist even after a relationship changes form.

As I continued to heal, I delved deeper into metaphysical healing, astrology, and spirituality. In my quest for knowledge and understanding, I decided to explore avenues

I had not considered before. I had always been curious but skeptical about spiritualists and their ability to connect with the other side. However, my curiosity led me to try it. I decided to meet with a spiritualist who came highly recommended, to see if I could connect with my parents, especially my mother, who had been gone the longest.

The experience with the spiritualist was unexpectedly profound and brought me immense comfort and a sense of connection that I had been missing. As she began the session, she shared details that no one outside of myself and God could have known. She spoke of specific memories and emotions that resonated deeply with me. Her descriptions of my father and our complicated relationship were eerily accurate, providing a sense of authenticity to the experience that I had not anticipated.

Through this connection, I felt my father's presence in a way I hadn't before. The spiritualist conveyed messages of regret and love from him, explaining that he had struggled with his demons and that his actions were never a reflection of his love for me. He even referred to me by my childhood nickname, Keke, which brought tears to my eyes.

My dad explained that his transition was painless and that his grandparents, my great-grandparents, came to get him. He apologized for leaving me and for not teaching me how men should treat me. He told me he saw everything that was going on in my life and assured me that he had been protecting both me and my son from the other side. He urged me to remember who I was during times of adversity and to continue fighting.

He shared memories of our past, recalling moments that only we knew about, which added to the authenticity of the experience. He expressed his sorrow for the times he was not there for me and acknowledged the pain his absence had caused. My father's messages were filled with love and remorse, and hearing him speak through the spiritualist brought a sense of closure and understanding that I had longed for.

He also told me that even though I often felt alone, I was not by myself. His presence was always with me, providing support and protection. The spiritualist sensed how heavy my energy was and shared that my dad could feel my heart was filled with grief, with holes and voids that no amount of good food, shopping, sex, or vices could heal. The biggest energy the spiritualist felt was my profound sense of loss.

I was not able to connect with my mother during this initial session, but after this experience, I was determined to try again. I scheduled a subsequent reading later, and finally, I was able to connect with her. Hearing from her after so many years brought a profound sense of serenity and joy. Her presence felt warm and nurturing, like a comforting embrace I had longed for.

She expressed her love and pride in me, encouraging me to continue my journey of healing and self-discovery. My mother also apologized for not being able to teach me how to love and value myself and not to base my happiness and worth on men. She acknowledged that I did not know how to be alone, and for some reason, that really got under my skin in a way that only a mother could. Her words cut deep, but they also illuminated a path towards understanding and growth that I had not seen before.

She mentioned that she had been watching everything I was doing and hated that I thought she was not there with me. She explained that a bird had been her way of getting my attention. A week before this reading, a bird flew into my balcony door and landed in my patio chair. I saw this bird up close and even took a picture of it. For whatever reason, at the time, I felt like the bird signaled something, but when she said it in the reading, it confirmed it.

My mother assured me she was not in any pain at the time of her transition, and the problem was with her heart, which is true. My mother said that although she misses living in a body, she is happy where she is and does not want me to think she is unhappy or not at peace. I was wondering to myself if she was at peace before the spiritualist shared that message. My mother shared that I needed to heal my heart and learn how to be alone. She felt that I allowed men to dishonor me, and she felt partly responsible for that because she was not here to show me.

In addition to my parents, I was able to connect with my late aunt Pat and my cousin Jerry, nicknamed "Wet," who even referred to himself by his nickname. Their messages were filled with love and encouragement, reminding me of the bonds that transcended physical existence. They shared stories and memories that brought both tears and laughter, reinforcing the sense of connection and support that I had been missing.

The spiritualist also helped me connect with my spirit guides, who provided guidance and support. Knowing that these benevolent forces were watching over me gave me a renewed sense of purpose and strength. It felt like a bridge had been built, connecting my past pain to my present healing. The spiritualist's insights allowed me to reconcile with the memories of my parents, understanding their struggles and their love in a new light. It was a spiritual awakening that brought a deep sense of calm and acceptance.

Reconnecting with my loved ones on the other side was a transformative experience. Just like in the movie "Ghost," my experience with the spiritualist offered a bridge between the past and the present, allowing for messages of love and reassurance to flow through, providing a sense of peace that words alone cannot describe. It provided a sense of closure and a deeper understanding of the love and protection that continued to surround me.

This journey of self-growth was not just about reconciling with the past; it was about embracing the present and looking forward to the future. I dived into activities and passions that I had long neglected and began my journey of self-love, holistic healing, and self-discovery. I started by meditating three to five times a day to connect with my heart and soul, God, my spirit guides, and deceased family. Through this practice, I started seeing that everything I had longed for so many years was already in me. I explored activities and passions that I had long neglected. Writing became a therapeutic outlet, a way to process my emotions and share my story, and it was this realization that inspired me to author my book.

Now, I find fulfillment in helping others who are navigating their own struggles. My relationships with friends and family deepened as I became more open and vulnerable; making my heart smile to connect on a more authentic level with those around me and see them heal loudly! This path was not just about finding peace within myself, but also about using my experiences to support and uplift those around me. This is why I went through these experiences and why God didn't allow me to check out of life—because I had a bigger purpose to fulfill by sharing my experiences and embracing my vulnerability to support and uplift others in their journeys.

Today, I am in a place of love, acceptance, peace, and serenity. The pain of the past no longer dictates my present because I know that everything that happened in my past happened FOR me, not TO me, and that I was not a victim of my circumstances but a victor! Through my journey of healing and personal growth, I had learned to find validation and love within myself and my Higher Power, rather than seeking it outside of me.

I was not always a believer in spiritualists, but this experience shattered my skepticism and opened my heart to new possibilities. This experience gave me a tool for healing and closure and helped me to see the true power lies within me and my ability to connect with my own spirit and inner guidance. It taught me that healing can come from the most unexpected places and that we are all divinely guided and supported even from beyond, and most importantly, that I was never alone!

If you are seeking closure from a deceased relative and don't believe in spiritual guidance, I would recommend finding ways to connect with their memory in a personal and meaningful way. This could involve writing letters to them, creating a memory book, or engaging in activities they loved. The key is to find a method that resonates with you and helps you process your emotions and find peace.

As I reflect on this journey of reconnection and rediscovery, I am filled with gratitude for the growth I've experienced and the insights I've gained. Each step of this process, from making amends to exploring spiritual connections, has contributed to my healing in ways I never expected. I've learned that healing is not just about overcoming past hurts, but about rediscovering who we truly are beneath the layers of pain and conditioning.

This journey has taught me that we are all connected - to each other, to those who have passed on, and to something greater than ourselves. It has shown me the power of forgiveness, both for others and for ourselves. And it has reinforced my belief in the resilience of the human spirit and our capacity for growth and transformation.

As I continue on this path, I carry with me the love and wisdom of those who have gone before, the support of those still with me, and a deepened connection to my own inner strength. I am no longer defined by my past, but empowered by the lessons it has taught me. And I am committed to using my experiences to help others find their own path to healing and self-discovery.

Remember, your path is unique, but you are not alone. There is healing, hope, and love available to you, sometimes in the most unexpected places. Trust in your path, be open to new experiences, and never underestimate the power of reconnecting - with others, with your past, and most importantly, with yourself.

Reflection Questions

1. How have you experienced closure or healing in relationships, even after someone has passed away?
2. In what ways have you reconnected with parts of yourself that you had neglected or forgotten?
3. How has your understanding of spirituality or connection to something greater than yourself evolved over time?
4. What unexpected sources of healing have you encountered in your life?
5. How do you nurture the parts of you that are still healing from long-standing pain?

Tips for Healing

1. Practice Open-mindedness: Be willing to explore new avenues of healing, even if they seem unconventional at first.

2. Cultivate Spiritual Connection: Whether through traditional religion, meditation, or connecting with nature, find ways to nurture your spiritual side.

3. Honor Your Intuition: Trust your inner voice and the signs that resonate with you personally.

4. Embrace Forgiveness: Work on forgiving others and yourself as a pathway to freedom and healing.

5. Share Your Story: Consider ways to use your experiences to help others, which can be deeply healing for you as well.

Healing Activity: Connection Ritual

Create a personal ritual to connect with loved ones who have passed or parts of yourself you want to reconnect with:

1. Choose a quiet, comfortable space where you won't be disturbed.
2. Light a candle or use an object that holds special meaning for you.
3. Take a few deep breaths to center yourself.

4. Speak aloud or write a letter expressing your feelings, asking questions, or sharing updates about your life.
5. Sit in silence for a few minutes, open to any thoughts or feelings that arise.
6. Close the ritual by expressing gratitude for the connection.

Repeat this ritual regularly or whenever you feel the need to reconnect.

Understanding Spiritual Healing and Connection

Spiritual healing and connection can play a significant role in emotional and psychological well-being:

1. Meaning and Purpose: Spiritual practices often provide a sense of meaning and purpose, which can be crucial in overcoming life's challenges.

2. Community Support: Many spiritual paths offer community support, providing a sense of belonging and shared experience.

3. Transcendence: Spiritual experiences can offer a sense of transcendence, helping individuals see beyond their immediate problems.

4. Emotional Regulation: Practices like meditation and prayer can aid in emotional regulation and stress reduction.

5. Forgiveness: Many spiritual traditions emphasize forgiveness, which can be a powerful tool for healing and moving forward.

6. Hope and Optimism: Spiritual beliefs often foster hope and optimism, which can be beneficial for mental health and resilience.

7. Coping Mechanism: Spirituality can provide coping mechanisms for dealing with life's difficulties and uncertainties.

8. Self-Reflection: Spiritual practices often encourage self-reflection, leading to greater self-awareness and personal growth.

9. Connection to Something Greater: The sense of being connected to something larger than oneself can provide comfort and reduce feelings of isolation.

10. Ritual and Routine: Spiritual rituals and routines can provide structure and stability, particularly during times of upheaval.

It's important to note that spiritual healing is deeply personal and what works for one person may not work for another. It's about finding what resonates with you and supports your healing journey. Whether through organized religion, personal spiritual practices, or a more general sense of connection to the universe, spiritual healing can be a powerful complement to other forms of therapy and self-care.

If you're interested in exploring spiritual healing, consider:

- Researching different spiritual traditions and practices
- Talking to spiritual leaders or counselors
- Joining spiritual or meditation groups
- Reading books on spirituality and healing
- Experimenting with different practices to see what feels right for you

Remember, the goal is to find practices that support your overall well-being and contribute positively to your healing journey.

Remember that healing is a journey of returning to your authentic self. It's about reconnecting with the parts of you that may have been lost or buried under pain and trauma. This process of rediscovery is ongoing, and each day brings new opportunities for growth and understanding.

Your experiences, both painful and joyful, have shaped you, but they do not define you. You have the power to rewrite your story, to forge new connections, and to discover new aspects of yourself. Trust in your journey, remain open to unexpected sources of healing, and never underestimate the power of connection - to others, to something greater than yourself, and most importantly, to your own inner wisdom.

As you move forward, carry with you the knowledge that you are supported, loved, and never truly alone. Your journey of healing and self-discovery has the power not only to transform your own life but to touch the lives of others around you. Each step you take towards wholeness ripples out into the world, creating possibilities for healing and growth far beyond what you might imagine.

Reconnecting isn't just about external relationships; it's also about reconnecting with the deepest parts of yourself. As you continue to rediscover who you are beyond your pain and past experiences, be gentle with yourself. Celebrate each moment of reconnection, no matter how small it may seem.

Your path of healing and rediscovery is uniquely yours, but you're not walking it alone. Whether through earthly relationships, spiritual connections, or the bond with your own higher self, you are supported on this journey. Trust in the process, remain open to new experiences, and know that every step forward is a victory worth celebrating.

As we close this chapter and look ahead, remember that the journey of reconnection and rediscovery is ongoing. Each day brings new opportunities to deepen your understanding of yourself and your place in the world. In the next chapter, we'll explore how to take the insights and growth you've gained and apply them to creating a life of purpose and fulfillment.

The road ahead may not always be easy, but you've already shown incredible strength and resilience. You have within you everything you need to continue this journey of healing and self-discovery. Trust in your path, embrace the support around you, and step boldly into the next phase of your journey, knowing that you are constantly evolving, growing, and becoming more authentically you.

Chapter 9
Journey Towards Healing

"True healing begins when we embrace our vulnerabilities and allow ourselves to be fully seen."

Taking the first step toward mental and emotional healing is one of the most courageous acts you can do for yourself. As I reflect on my own journey, I'm reminded of the day I finally admitted to myself that I needed help. It was a pivotal moment, one that required honesty, patience, and a willingness to face parts of myself I had long kept hidden. I had spent so many years convincing myself that I was strong enough to carry it all—my burdens, my pain—but that moment of admission was the first time I truly understood that strength could also mean surrendering, letting go, and allowing myself to be supported.

Healing is deeply personal and requires you to be honest, patient, accepting, courageous, trusting, and resilient. Every small step forward is a victory, and I want to share with you the insights and framework that have helped me along the way. Healing is not just about feeling better — it is about transforming my life, confronting the deepest parts of myself that I had avoided for so long, and learning to live with authenticity. And that kind of healing is never easy.

Admitting Struggles

The first and most crucial step is admitting that your life has become unmanageable, and your emotions are overwhelming you. Recognizing that you cannot manage this on your own is liberating. It opens the door to receiving help and support from others.

For me, this admission came after years of trying to handle everything on my own. I remember the weight lifting from my shoulders as I finally said out loud, "I need help." It was scary, but it was also the first step towards real change. That moment wasn't just about admitting defeat; it was about finding the strength to admit that I deserved more than just surviving — I deserved to thrive.

Finding Hope

Believe that change is possible. Seek out stories of others who have overcome similar challenges and find hope in their journeys. Surround yourself with positive influences and believe in the possibility of a better future for yourself. When I first attended an Emotions Anonymous meeting, hearing others share their stories of recovery was like finding a map in a dark forest. Their words whispered, "If they can do it, so can I." This hope became a lifeline, pulling me forward even on my darkest days. There were moments when hope was the only thing keeping me from falling apart, and it reminded me that even in the depths of despair, there was always a possibility of light.

Seeking Guidance

Reach out to professionals, mentors, and supportive friends. Their insights and advice can help you navigate the complexities of your emotions and begin to heal. Remember, seeking help is a sign of strength, not weakness.

My experience with therapy taught me the value of professional guidance. Having someone to help me unpack my emotions and experiences provided clarity I couldn't find on my own. It's okay to try different therapists or types of therapy until you find what works for you. I remember feeling vulnerable, afraid that I would never find someone who truly understood me. But the act of seeking guidance was transformative; it showed me that I didn't have to have all the answers—I just needed to be willing to ask for help.

Self-Reflection

Take an honest look at your life and identify the areas that need change. Reflect on your past actions and behaviors that have contributed to your current state. This self-reflection will help you understand yourself better and identify the root causes of your struggles. Through journaling and meditation, I began to see patterns in my behavior that I had never noticed before. This awareness was sometimes painful, but it was necessary for growth. Each realization became a stepping stone on my path to healing. The deeper I reflected, the more I began to uncover hidden layers of my past—wounds I hadn't even known were still open. The process wasn't linear, and sometimes it felt overwhelming to confront these buried emotions, but with each discovery, I reclaimed a piece of myself.

Admitting Faults

Acknowledge your mistakes and take responsibility for your actions. Holding onto guilt and shame hinders your progress. By admitting your faults, you can release some of the burdens you carry and pave the way for healing.

This step was particularly challenging for me. Admitting the ways I had hurt others and myself required a level of vulnerability I wasn't used to. But with each admission, I felt lighter, more authentic, and more capable of change. Guilt had always been a companion in my life, but I learned that it could only hold me prisoner for as long as I allowed it to.

Seek Forgiveness & Apologize

Part of healing involves seeking forgiveness from those you have hurt, including yourself. Reach out to those you have wronged, express your sincere apologies, and ask for their forgiveness. Understand that the other person may not forgive you, but what matters is that you are forgiving yourself. Making amends helps rebuild trust and fosters healthier relationships. The process of making amends taught me about the power of genuine apology and the freedom that comes with forgiveness – both given and received. It wasn't easy, but it was an essential part of my healing journey.

It also helped me understand that forgiveness doesn't erase the past, but it does free us from its grip. Forgiving myself, in particular, was the hardest part, but it was the key to unlocking the next phase of my healing.

Continuous Self-Improvement

Commit to continuous self-improvement. Set goals, learn new skills, and embrace personal development. By focusing on ongoing improvement, you keep moving forward on your healing journey.

For me, this meant reading self-help books, attending workshops, and constantly challenging myself to step out of my comfort zone. Each new skill or insight I gained felt like adding a tool to my emotional toolkit, equipping me better for life's challenges. There were moments when I resisted growth, afraid of what it might mean to leave behind people and the version of myself I had grown so used to. But I realized that growth requires letting go, and with each step, I was becoming someone I could finally be proud of.

Spiritual Connection

Connecting with a higher power or a sense of spirituality can be an integral part of healing. This connection provides strength, guidance, and a sense of purpose. Whether through prayer, meditation, or other spiritual practices, this aspect can help you find inner peace and resilience.

My own spiritual journey involved exploring various practices before finding what resonated with me. I found comfort in meditation, connection in nature, and guidance through prayer. This spiritual dimension added depth to my healing, helping me find meaning in my struggles and hope for the future. In moments of uncertainty, my spiritual connection became an anchor, grounding me in something larger than myself.

Support Others

As you progress in your healing, recognize the importance of supporting others on similar journeys. Sharing your experiences and offering support to those struggling helps reinforce your own growth and healing.

When I began to share my story and offer support to others, I found a new sense of purpose. It was as if my pain now had meaning – it became a tool to help others find hope and healing. This act of service not only benefited others but also continued to fuel my own recovery. Knowing that my journey could provide comfort to someone else transformed my pain into a source of empowerment.

Practice Gratitude

Focus on the positive aspects of your life and express gratitude for your blessings. Practicing gratitude daily can help you maintain a positive outlook and foster a sense of contentment.

I started a gratitude journal, writing down three things I was thankful for each day. At first, it was challenging to find things to be grateful for, but over time, this practice shifted my perspective. I began to look for the good and appreciate the small joys in life, which gradually changed my overall outlook. Gratitude became my compass on tough days when all I could see was darkness, reminding me of the light that still existed in my world.

Live On Purpose

Find meaning in your experiences and use them to fuel your passion for helping others. Embracing your purpose gives you direction and motivation to live on purpose, allowing you to live a fulfilling and impactful life.

For me, this meant using my experiences with mental health struggles to become an advocate for others facing similar challenges. It gave my past pain a purpose and helped me transform my struggles into a source of strength and inspiration for others. Living on purpose has become my guiding star — knowing that I am here for a reason has filled my life with a sense of meaning that I never imagined possible.

Remember, the journey towards healing is not linear. There will be setbacks and challenges along the way. But each step forward, no matter how small, is progress. Be patient with yourself, celebrate your victories, and know that you are worthy of healing and happiness.

Your journey towards healing is uniquely yours, but you are not alone on this path. There are others who have walked similar roads and found their way to healing. Let their stories inspire you, let the support of others guide you, and let your own inner strength propel you forward.

As you continue on this path of healing, remember that you are not defined by your past or your struggles. You are a resilient, evolving being capable of transformation and growth. Embrace this journey with an open heart and a willingness to learn and grow. The road may be challenging, but the destination – a life of authenticity, peace, and fulfillment – is worth every step.

Reflection Questions

1. What areas of your life do you feel need the most healing? How can you take a small step towards addressing these areas today?

2. How has asking for help changed your healing process and sense of self? What new insights have you gained about your own healing process?

3. In what ways have you seen growth or positive change in yourself, even in the midst of challenges?

4. How can you incorporate gratitude into your daily life? What are three things you're grateful for right now?

5. What does living "on purpose" mean to you? How can you align your daily actions with your sense of purpose?

Tips for Healing

1. Recognize the Power of Vulnerability: Acknowledge that opening up allows for deeper connections and a more authentic self.

2. Release the Need to Control: Let go of the idea that you must carry your burdens alone — there's strength in community.

3. Create an Emotional Toolkit: Equip yourself with resources like journaling, breathwork, or therapy that support emotional resilience.

4. Find Comfort in Your Journey: Trust the process, even in moments of uncertainty — healing isn't linear.

5. Celebrate Small Victories: Acknowledge and celebrate every step forward, no matter how small it may seem.

As we conclude this chapter, remember that your healing journey is a testament to your strength and resilience. Every step you take towards healing is an act of courage and self-love. Trust in your ability to heal, grow, and transform. You have within you everything you need to create a life of authenticity, peace, and fulfillment.

The road ahead may have its challenges, but you are not walking it alone. There are countless others on similar journeys, and together, we create a tapestry of healing that extends far beyond our individual experiences. Your healing not only transforms your life but has the power to inspire and uplift others.

As you move forward, carry with you the knowledge that you are worthy of love, respect, and happiness. Your past does not define you, and your future is full of possibility. Embrace your journey with open arms, knowing that each day brings new opportunities for growth, connection, and joy.

Chapter 10
Taking It One Day at a Time

"Healing is a journey, not a destination. Each day is a step forward, no matter how small."

As I sit here reflecting on my journey, I'm struck by a profound realization: healing isn't about reaching a final destination. It's about embracing each step of the journey, no matter how small or seemingly insignificant. This understanding didn't come easily. It was born from countless moments of frustration, setbacks, and the gradual acceptance that true healing unfolds one day at a time.

I remember a particularly challenging day about a year into my recovery. I had been making steady progress, attending my therapy sessions regularly and feeling more stable than I had in years. Then, out of nowhere, a wave of anxiety hit me. It was as if all my hard work had evaporated in an instant. I found myself curled up on my bathroom floor, struggling to breathe, convinced that I was back at square one.

In that moment of despair, I recalled something my therapist had told me: "*Keana, healing isn't linear. There will be ups and downs, but each day is a step forward, even if it doesn't feel like it.*" Those words became my lifeline. I took a deep breath, stood up, and decided to focus on getting through just that one day. It wasn't about erasing all my progress; it was about acknowledging my struggle and choosing to keep moving forward one small step at a time.

This experience taught me the importance of patience and commitment in the healing process. There will be days when you feel on top of the world, capable of conquering anything. But there will also be days when it feels like you've regressed, when the weight of your past seems overwhelming. It's crucial to understand that both types of days are part of the journey.

On my good days, I learned to celebrate every victory, no matter how small. Getting out of bed, making a healthy meal, or reaching out to a friend became achievements worth acknowledging. These small wins built momentum and encouraged me to keep moving forward.

On my hardest days, I had to practice something that felt foreign to me — self-compassion. I had spent so long being my own harshest critic, pushing myself to always "do better" or "be stronger." But I began to understand that true strength doesn't come from being unbreakable. It comes from being able to break and still find the courage to put yourself back together. I reminded myself that one bad day didn't erase the progress I had made. Instead of berating myself for struggling, I treated myself with the same kindness and understanding I would offer a friend. I learned that bad days don't define the entirety of my journey.

There were days when the urge to isolate myself felt almost impossible to resist. I would tell myself that I was a burden to others, and that my struggles were mine alone to carry. I convinced myself that no one could possibly understand the depth of my pain. But I soon realized that this thinking only pushed me deeper into the darkness. Over time, I began to understand that leaning on my support network wasn't a sign of weakness — it was a sign of strength. Reaching out, even when I felt unworthy of love, was an act of courage. Whether it was leaning on friends, family, my therapist, or EA sponsor their presence helped keep me anchored when my inner world felt too chaotic to manage alone.

One tool that has been invaluable in my healing process is setting realistic goals. I used to overwhelm myself with grand expectations, thinking I needed to transform my entire life overnight. This approach inevitably led to disappointment and feelings of failure. Now, I break down my recovery into small, manageable goals. Each day, I set an intention, something achievable that contributes to my overall well-being.

For instance, one day my goal might be to practice mindfulness for five minutes. Another day, it could be to reach out to a supportive friend or try a new healthy recipe. These small steps, taken consistently, have created a foundation for lasting change and healing.

I've also learned the importance of staying connected. Surrounding myself with a supportive network of friends, family, and fellow recovery warriors has been crucial. There were times when I wanted to isolate myself, convinced that I was a burden to others. But I've found that sharing my journey, both the triumphs and the struggles, has not only provided me with encouragement and accountability but has also allowed me to support others in their healing.

Incorporating holistic recovery techniques into my daily routine has been another game-changer. I discovered that healing involves more than just addressing my mental health; it requires nurturing my body and spirit as well. Mindfulness and meditation have become daily practices, helping me stay grounded and bringing clarity to my thoughts. Even on my busiest days, I make time for a few minutes of deep breathing or a short, guided meditation. Physical movement has also played a crucial role in my recovery.

Some days, this means a vigorous workout or a long walk in nature. On harder days, it might be as simple as some gentle stretching or a short yoga session. The key is to listen to my body and honor what it needs each day.

Expressing myself creatively has been another powerful outlet. Writing and journaling, in particular, have been transformative for me. Journaling has allowed me to not only process my emotions but also track my growth over time. It gave me the opportunity to reflect deeply on my experiences, and it was through my journals and personal memories that I was able to write this book. On days when I feel stuck, I can look back and see how far I've come, reminding myself that progress is possible even if it's not always visible in the moment.

One practice that has significantly shifted my mindset is the use of positive affirmations. I've placed these affirmations around my home, on my phone, and in my journal. Phrases like "I am worthy of love and healing" and "Each day brings new opportunities for growth" serve as constant reminders of my strength and resilience. These affirmations have slowly but surely reshaped my internal dialogue, replacing self-doubt with self-compassion and hope.

Throughout this journey, I've learned that seeking professional help is not a sign of weakness but a testament to my commitment to healing. There have been times when I've needed additional support, and reaching out to my therapist or counselor has provided valuable insights and tools for managing my mental health.

Handling setbacks or relapses has been one of the most challenging aspects of healing. I've had to learn to acknowledge these moments without self-judgment, using them as opportunities for learning and growth. When I experience a setback, I lean on my support system, engage in self-care practices, and revisit the tools and strategies that have helped me in the past.

There were moments when I doubted my ability to keep going, when the weight of the journey felt overwhelming. But over time, I redefined what success looked like for me. Success wasn't about never having another bad day — it was about continuing to show up for myself, even when I didn't feel strong. It was about recognizing the progress I had made, even when setbacks made it hard to see.

To those of you on your own healing journey, I want to emphasize the importance of being gentle with yourself. Seek support when you need it, and remember that setbacks are a natural part of the process. Keep moving forward, one step at a time. Your journey is uniquely yours, and it's not about how fast you reach your destination but about the growth and resilience you develop along the way.

Remember, you are not alone on this journey. I am here with you, as are countless others who understand your struggles and triumphs. Together, we can create a world where mental health is prioritized, vulnerability is embraced, and everyone feels empowered to take the first step toward healing and growth.

As we close this chapter, I invite you to reflect on your own journey. Acknowledge how far you've come, recognize the strength and resilience you possess, and reaffirm your commitment to your healing path. What steps can you take today to support your well-being? How can you show yourself compassion and patience?

Remember, healing is a journey of small steps, daily choices, and unwavering commitment to yourself. Embrace each day as an opportunity for growth, and trust that with time and perseverance, you will continue to move forward on your path to healing and self-discovery.

Reflection Questions

1. How do you currently handle setbacks or challenging days in your healing journey? What strategies have been most effective for you?

2. What small, achievable goals can you set for yourself this week to support your healing and recovery?

3. How can you incorporate more self-compassion into your daily life, especially on difficult days?

4. How do you remind yourself to stay present and focus on today, instead of worrying about the future?

5. Reflect on a recent victory in your healing journey, no matter how small. How did this success make you feel, and what did it teach you about your own resilience?

Tips for Healing

1. Focus on the Present: Stay grounded by focusing on what you can control today, rather than worrying about the future.

2. Create a Gratitude Ritual: Each night, write down three things you're grateful for. This practice can shift your focus to the positive aspects of your life.

3. Establish a Support System: Identify trusted friends, family members, or support groups you can reach out to on challenging days.

4. Be Patient with Yourself: Healing takes time — give yourself permission to go at your own pace.

5. Develop Healthy Coping Mechanisms: Find positive ways to deal with stress and difficult emotions, such as deep breathing exercises, journaling, or engaging in your favorite hobby.

Your healing journey is uniquely yours. Honor your process, be patient with yourself, and trust that each day brings you one step closer to the peace and wholeness you seek.

Chapter 11
The Multitudes of Healing

"Healing is not just mending the broken parts; it's creating a new whole."

As I continued on my journey of recovery, I began to understand that healing is far more complex and multifaceted than I had initially believed. It's not just about addressing one aspect of our lives or fixing a single issue. True healing, I discovered, involves nurturing every part of ourselves - our minds, our bodies, our spirits, and our connections with others.

I remember the day this realization truly hit home. I was sitting in my therapist's office, feeling frustrated. "I've been doing everything right," I said, my voice tight with emotion. "I'm taking my medication, I'm attending therapy, I'm even exercising regularly. So why do I still feel like something's missing?

My therapist smiled gently and asked, "Keana, when you think about healing, what does that look like to you?"

Her question caught me off guard. I had to pause and really think about it. For so long, I had viewed healing as simply a matter of getting rid of pain — whether physical, emotional, or mental. I began to understand that I had been viewing my healing as a purely mental health issue. But the truth was, my journey towards wholeness encompassed so much more.

Healing is so much more than just fixing what's broken. It's about finding a new way to exist, a new sense of wholeness that wasn't dependent on erasing the scars of the past but learning how to live with them in a healthy way. I also realized that much of my internal struggle came from a disconnection between my heart and mind. My heart was burdened with grief, trauma, and unresolved pain, while my mind tried desperately to rationalize or dismiss these feelings. This constant tug-of-war left me feeling fragmented, and it became clear that true healing would only come when my heart and mind were in harmony — when they both aligned with my soul's deeper truth.

This conversation marked the beginning of a new phase in my healing journey - one where I started to explore and nurture different aspects of my well-being. Healing, I realized, wasn't just a singular act. It was multitudes. Let me share with you what I've learned about the multitudes of healing:

Emotional Healing

Emotional healing became a cornerstone of my journey. For years, I lived under a misdiagnosis of bipolar disorder, a label that didn't reflect my true reality but profoundly shaped how I saw myself and approached my mental health.

This is not to negate or diminish the experiences of those who live with bipolar disorder. Their struggles are valid, and their stories deserve to be heard with empathy and respect. The misdiagnosis added to my sense of confusion and disconnection, keeping me from understanding the deeper emotional wounds at the root of my struggles. It wasn't just about managing symptoms; it was about learning to process and release negative emotions, finding forgiveness—especially for myself—and cultivating a sense of inner peace.

This disconnection between my heart and mind only added to the chaos. My heart was screaming out for healing, for acknowledgment, but my mind kept rationalizing it away, telling me that if I just "did better" or "worked harder," everything would be okay. This misalignment was a major source of my mental health challenges. Once I started allowing my heart and mind to work together — to process emotions rather than fight against them — I felt a shift. I began to realize that my mental health couldn't improve until I addressed the emotional wounds that were crying out to be heard.

I carried so much unresolved hurt and often found myself stuck in a cycle of self-blame. The weight of my past choices and mistakes haunted me, and every moment of joy was shadowed by guilt. I found it hard to forgive myself for the wrongs I had done. But one thing I learned in EA is that forgiveness isn't about excusing your behavior — it's about releasing yourself from the shackles of shame.

Forgiving others who had hurt me was challenging, but I found that forgiving myself was even harder. I had to let go of the guilt and shame I carried for past actions and mistakes. It was a gradual process, but with each small act of self-forgiveness, I felt a little lighter, a little more at peace. Slowly, painfully, I learned to forgive myself — not because I had done everything right, but because I was worthy of the same grace I extended to others.

One practice that significantly helped my emotional healing was journaling. Each evening, I would spend time writing about my feelings, both positive and negative. This act of putting my emotions on paper helped me acknowledge them without judgment and begin to understand their roots. There was something cathartic about seeing my pain written out — it made it feel less overwhelming, more manageable. As if, in those pages, I could control my narrative instead of feeling like a prisoner to it.

Mental Healing

Mental healing involved reframing negative thoughts, managing stress, and developing a more positive mindset. Cognitive Behavioral Therapy (CBT) played a crucial role in this aspect of my healing. Through CBT, I learned to identify negative thought patterns and replace them with more balanced, realistic ones.

This disconnection between my heart and mind had played a major role in my mental health struggles. My heart was yearning for healing, weighed down by unresolved grief and emotional pain, while my mind was stuck in a loop of negative thoughts, trying to rationalize it all away. The misalignment created inner chaos, leaving me at war with myself. Once I began to acknowledge both my heart and mind — to let them work together in harmony — I started to feel a profound shift in my mental health.

My mind was often my biggest enemy. I had become so used to spiraling into thoughts of worthlessness and despair that I didn't even notice when it was happening. CBT helped me catch those thoughts in real time and gave me tools to challenge them. It wasn't easy — sometimes it felt like I was constantly at war with my own mind — but slowly, I began to shift my thinking. I began to realize that I wasn't defined by my darkest moments. Healing didn't mean never having those thoughts again — it meant knowing I could survive them.

I also discovered the power of mindfulness in promoting mental healing. By allowing my mind to quiet, I could hear the truth my heart had been trying to tell me all along: that I needed to heal, not just mentally, but emotionally. Practicing mindfulness helped me stay grounded in the present moment, rather than getting lost in anxieties about the future or regrets about the past. Starting my day with a short mindfulness meditation became a ritual that set a positive tone for the hours ahead.

Physical Healing

I came to understand that my physical health was intricately connected to my mental and emotional well-being. As I began to heal emotionally and mentally, I realized how much I had been asking of myself without offering my body the care and attention it needed. Taking care of my body through proper nutrition, regular exercise, and adequate rest became an essential part of my healing journey. When my heart, mind, and body began to align, I felt a balance I hadn't experienced in years.

I started small, with daily walks around my neighborhood. As I built strength and confidence, I explored different forms of exercise until I found activities I genuinely enjoyed. Yoga, in particular, became a powerful tool for me, combining physical movement with mindfulness and breathwork. The practice not only strengthened my body but also allowed me to reconnect with my breath, with each inhale and exhale grounding me in the present moment.

Nutrition also played a crucial role. I learned about the gut-brain connection and how the foods we eat can impact our mood and mental health. Gradually, I started making healthier food choices, noticing improvements not just in my physical health but in my overall sense of well-being. By nourishing my body, I was able to create a sense of harmony between my physical state and the healing journey of my heart and mind.

Spiritual Healing

Spiritual healing was an unexpected but profound part of my journey. It wasn't about adhering to a specific religion, but rather about connecting with something greater than myself and finding a sense of purpose and meaning in my life. This connection was vital to healing the deep wounds in my soul that had been ignored for so long. I realized that healing could never be complete without addressing the spiritual disconnection between my mind, heart, and soul.

For me, this transformative shift took place during a spiritual retreat in Sedona, AZ. Surrounded by the red rocks and powerful vortexes, I began to explore deeper layers of healing — ones that extended beyond my physical and emotional pain. One particularly powerful moment came during a solo hike. As I stood at the top of a hill, overlooking a vast, breathtaking landscape, I felt a deep sense of peace and belonging. It was as if, for the first time, I could see my place in the grand tapestry of life. The disconnection I had felt for so long, the emptiness I had tried to fill with external validation, began to fade.

This experience reinforced my belief in the healing power of nature and spirituality. I had always searched for something outside of myself to bring me peace, but now I was learning that peace had been inside me all along — I just had to uncover it by aligning my heart and mind with my soul. In reconnecting with my soul, I began to feel a new sense of belonging in the world and the collective. This newfound connection brought a sense of harmony and purpose that I had long been missing.

Practicing meditation, spending time in nature, and exploring different philosophical and spiritual teachings further solidified this sense of inner connection. These practices helped me gain perspective on my struggles and fostered a sense of connection to the world around me. The healing I had sought for so long wasn't something I needed to find externally; it was a journey of uncovering what had always been within.

Social Healing

Finally, I learned about the importance of social healing — building and maintaining healthy relationships and finding a supportive community. This aspect of healing was challenging for me, as my struggles had often led me to isolate myself from others. I had spent so long disconnected from those around me that the thought of reaching out and making myself vulnerable felt overwhelming. Yet, I began to realize that healing wasn't something I could do in isolation. Gradually, I began to reconnect with friends and family, being honest about my journey and my needs. I also sought out support groups where I could connect with others who understood my experiences. These connections became a vital source of support, understanding, and encouragement.

In reconnecting with people, I began to feel a new sense of belonging in the world and the collective. For so long, I had seen my pain as something isolating, something that set me apart from others. But through these relationships, I started to understand that we are all interconnected and that healing doesn't happen in isolation — it happens within the community. This collective support helped me feel more grounded in both my personal healing and my place in the larger world.

I remember the first time I shared my story at a support group meeting. My voice shook, and my hands trembled, but as I spoke, I saw nods of understanding and empathy from around the room. In that moment, I felt a profound sense of belonging and acceptance. It was a powerful reminder that we are not alone in our struggles and that there is strength in shared experiences.

By reconnecting with others, I realized that healing is not only an individual journey but also a communal one. These bonds of support and shared understanding became integral to my recovery, reinforcing the importance of social healing in my overall well-being.

Practicing Healing

Understanding these different aspects of healing was just the first step. The real work came in putting this knowledge into practice in my daily life. I had to be intentional about incorporating healing into every aspect of my routine. This was not just about addressing one area of my life — it was about aligning my mind, heart, and soul with my desire to heal. Here are some of the strategies I found most helpful:

1. **Acknowledge Your Pain**: I learned to recognize and accept my pain without judgment. Acknowledgment is necessary for healing to begin. It's a way of saying, "Yes, this hurts, but I can survive this."

2. **Seek Professional Help**: Therapists, counselors, and support groups provided invaluable guidance and support throughout my journey. Healing is not a solitary journey — it's one that benefits from professional guidance and communal support.

3. **Build a Support Network**: Surrounding myself with supportive people was crucial. Knowing I wasn't alone, and that others genuinely cared about my well-being, gave me strength on days when healing felt impossible.

4. **Practice Self-Care**: I prioritized activities that nurtured my mind, body, and spirit, from relaxing baths to hobbies I enjoyed. Each act of self-care reminded me I was worth the effort, and deserving of love, nurturing, and care.

5. **Set Realistic Goals:** Breaking my healing into small, manageable steps helped me stay motivated and see progress. Small victories, like attending therapy or getting out of bed on hard days, showed me healing was happening, even when it didn't feel like it.

6. **Express Yourself:** Writing and sharing my story with others became powerful tools for processing my emotions. Turning my pain into something visible helped me release it in ways that words alone couldn't.

7. **Stay Positive:** Focusing on positive affirmations and surrounding myself with reminders of hope, like pictures and uplifting quotes, helped shift my mindset. These small visual cues became beacons of light on dark days.

8. **Be Patient:** I learned that healing takes time. It's not linear, and there were moments I wanted to fast-forward through the pain. But I had to give myself grace, accept setbacks, and keep moving forward, even when progress felt slow.

As I reflect on my journey, I'm in awe of how far I've come. The path hasn't been easy, and there have been many setbacks along the way. But by embracing these multitudes of healing - emotional, mental, physical, spiritual, and social - I've discovered a sense of wholeness I never thought possible. The alignment of my mind, body, and soul has become my compass, guiding me through the dark moments and reminding me of my capacity to heal.

Remember, your healing journey is uniquely yours. What works for one person may not work for another. Be patient with yourself as you explore different aspects of healing, and don't be afraid to seek help when you need it. You are on a brave and beautiful journey towards wholeness, and every step you take is a victory worth celebrating.

Reflection Questions

1. Which aspect of healing (emotional, mental, physical, spiritual, or social) do you feel needs the most attention in your life right now? Why?

2. Can you recall a moment when you experienced healing in an unexpected way? What did this teach you about your journey?

3. How have your relationships with others impacted your healing process? Are there ways you could foster more supportive connections?

4. In what ways have you learned to balance multiple areas of healing at the same time?

5. How do you stay present with the complexity of healing without feeling overwhelmed?

Tips for Holistic Healing

1. Practice Mindful Breathing: Take a few minutes each day to focus on your breath. This simple act can center you and reduce stress.

2. Nurture Your Body: Make one small change to better care for your physical health, whether it's drinking more water, taking a daily walk, or choosing a nutritious snack.

3. Create Holistic Practices: Incorporate practices that nurture all parts of yourself, such as meditation, journaling, and physical care.

4. Connect with Nature: Spend time outdoors regularly, even if it's just sitting in a nearby park. Nature has a powerful ability to calm and heal.

5. Explore Creativity: Try a new creative activity, whether it's coloring, writing, singing, or dancing. Creative expression can be deeply therapeutic.

Healing is a journey, not a destination. Embrace each aspect of your being as you move towards wholeness, and know that every small step is progress. You are capable of profound healing and growth, and you deserve to experience the peace and joy that comes with it.

Chapter 12
A Personal Letter to My Soulmates

"Awakened by the journey, we carry forward the light and live these lessons in every part of our lives."

My Dear Soulmates,

As I sit down to write this final chapter, my heart is overflowing with gratitude and love for each of you. This journey we've shared through these pages has been deeply personal and transformative, not just for me, but I hope for you as well. I want to speak to you directly, from my heart to yours, because you matter, and your life is profoundly important.

I remember the day I decided to write this book. I was sitting in my favorite coffee shop, a place I often retreated to when I needed to think. As I sipped my honey citrus mint tea, I reflected on my journey – the pain, the struggles, the moments of despair, but also the triumphs, the growth, and the unexpected joys.

In that moment, I realized that my story wasn't just mine to keep. It wasn't just a collection of experiences that would fade into memory. It was a testament to the resilience of the human spirit, a beacon of hope for those still struggling in the darkness. I knew that by sharing my experiences, I could potentially reach out to someone who felt as lost and alone as I once did. And that idea gave me the strength I needed to begin writing.

There have been moments in my life when I felt utterly alone, drowning in despair, and convinced that there was no way out. I know how it feels to be overwhelmed by the weight of grief, depression, and hopelessness. I know what it's like to feel as though the world is closing in, and the darkness is impenetrable. It feels endless, doesn't it? Like you're trapped in a void no one else can see or feel. I spent so many nights questioning my worth, wondering if my existence even mattered.

I vividly recall one particularly dark night years ago, shortly after moving into my new home, when the pain felt unbearable. I stood at the edge of a precipice, both literally and figuratively, questioning whether my life had any value at all. That moment felt like a crossroads — a terrifying place where I could either let go or hold on. But something, a small but undeniable force, held me back — a tiny flicker of hope, a whisper in my heart that said, *"Not yet. Your story isn't over."* I didn't know it then, but that whisper was the first step toward reclaiming my life.

That's why I'm here today, writing to you, to tell you that even in those darkest moments, there is a glimmer of light, a spark of hope, and a reason to keep going. You matter. Your presence in this world makes a difference. The pain you feel right now is real, but it does not define you. It is a chapter in your story, not the entire book.

If there's one thing, I want you to take from my journey, it's this: You have within you the strength to overcome, the resilience to rise, and the courage to keep moving forward — even when it feels impossible. You are not alone in this journey; we are in this together, walking side by side.

There were times when I wanted to give up, times when I questioned whether my life had any value, whether it was worth continuing to fight. I've been in that space where it feels like the weight of the world is crushing your chest, making it hard to breathe, hard to think, hard to believe there's anything better ahead. But somehow, I found my way through by holding on to the belief that my life had meaning, that my struggles were not in vain. It wasn't easy—nothing about this process ever is—but it was worth it. And so is your life. So are you!

One of the greatest lessons I've learned through this journey is the importance of embracing our feelings instead of running from them. Pain, sadness, and grief are part of the human experience, and it's okay to allow yourself to feel them fully. There's no shame in crying, no weakness in admitting that you're hurting. Grief, in particular, needs space—it deserves to be acknowledged. Trying to suppress your emotions only prolongs the healing process. When we embrace what we feel, we start to move through it, rather than staying stuck in it.

I found solace in the love of my son, in the support of my friends and family, and in the belief that I could turn my pain into purpose. I found solace in the love of my son, the support of my friends and family, and the belief that I could turn my pain into purpose. There is immense power in turning your wounds into wisdom, in allowing your struggles to fuel your growth rather than hold you back.

I also learned the power of asking for help, even when it felt difficult. For so long, I believed that I had to carry my burdens alone, that reaching out for support was a sign of weakness. But the truth is, asking for help takes immense courage. It is an act of strength to recognize when you need support and to use your voice to ask for it. Whether it's a trusted friend, a family member, or a professional, let them in. You don't have to walk this road alone. We are meant to lean on each other. You deserve to be supported, heard, and understood.

Never give up on yourself. I know it might seem like the easier choice when faced with overwhelming pain and challenges. But the truth is, giving up deprives you of the opportunity to witness the beauty and strength that can emerge from your struggles. Trust me when I say that the person you'll become on the other side of this pain is someone extraordinary ways you can't yet imagine.

Every challenge you face is a chance to grow. Each obstacle builds your resilience, shapes your character, and strengthens your spirit. You may not always see it, but Your life touches others in profound ways. Your strength has the power to uplift and inspire those around you, just as you've been lifted by others who walked this path before you.

I know it's hard to see past the pain, but remember that life is full of unexpected twists. What feels unbearable now might lead to incredible moments of incredible joy and opportunity for tomorrow. Sometimes, it's the darkest moments that make us look inward and discover our true selves. It's in those moments that you learn who you really are, and what you're truly capable of.

Your presence and love matter more than you might realize. Your painful experiences can become a source of purpose and meaning. You can use them to help others and make a difference in ways you can't even imagine right now. There is always hope for healing, no matter how dire things may seem. Time, support, and the right resources can lead to recovery and peace.

Overcoming your struggles is a personal victory that no one can take away from you. It's a testament to your strength and resilience. And with each passing day, you will grow stronger, even when it feels like the opposite. That strength will carry you forward, and in time, you'll see how far you've come.

Perspectives change with time and healing. What feels impossible now may look entirely different in the future. By not giving up, you leave a legacy of strength and resilience for others to follow. You create a ripple effect, one that has the power to change the world in small but significant ways. Every day is a new chance to make amends, forgive yourself, and start anew. You are part of something bigger than yourself, and your life has a unique purpose that only you can fulfill.

As we conclude this journey together, I want you to know that your healing journey is a testament to your strength and resilience. Every step you take towards healing is an act of courage and self-love. Trust in your ability to heal, grow, and transform. You have within you everything you need to create a life of authenticity, peace, and fulfillment.

The road ahead may have its challenges, but you are not walking it alone. There are countless others on similar journeys, and together, we create a tapestry of healing that extends far beyond our individual experiences. Your healing not only transforms your life but has the power to inspire and uplift others, to light the way for someone who may feel lost right now.

As you move forward, remember that you are worthy of love, respect, and happiness. Your past does not define your future; the possibilities ahead are endless. Embrace your journey, knowing that each day brings new opportunities for growth, connection, and joy. In moments of doubt, when the darkness feels overwhelming, remember this: you are loved, you are needed, and your life has purpose. Hold on to that truth, and let it guide you through the storm. Together, we can create a world where mental health is prioritized, where vulnerability is embraced, and where everyone feels empowered to heal and grow.

Thank you for allowing me to share my story with you. Thank you for being a part of this journey. You are my soulmates, and I am here with you, every step of the way. Never forget that you are loved, you are needed, and your life has purpose.

Remember, take it one day at a time. Your journey is uniquely yours, but you are never alone. Keep moving forward, keep believing in yourself, and keep spreading the light of your healing to others.

With all my love and deepest respect,

Keana

Reflection Questions

1. What part of my letter resonated most strongly with you? Why do you think it had such an impact?
2. How has your perspective on your own journey changed after reading this book?
3. What is one promise you can make to yourself today to honor your healing journey?
4. How can you use your own experiences to support and inspire others who might be struggling?

5. What does "never give up on you" mean to you personally? How can you embody this message in your daily life?

Final Thoughts for Your Journey

1. Embrace Your Uniqueness: Your journey is yours alone. Honor it, learn from it, and let it shape you into the beautiful, resilient person you are meant to be.

2. Embrace Your Feelings: Don't shy away from sadness, anger, or grief. Allow yourself to feel, and trust that through those feelings comes healing.

3. Ask for Help: It's okay to ask for support. Use your voice to seek out the people who can stand beside you when you need them the most.

4. Practice Self-Compassion: Be gentle with yourself, especially on difficult days. Healing is not a straight line. Treat yourself with the same kindness and understanding you'd offer a dear friend. You are worthy of that love.

5. Celebrate Every Victory: No step forward is too small to celebrate. Acknowledge your progress, no matter how insignificant it may seem.

6. Stay Connected: Reach out to others, share your story, and allow yourself to be supported. We are stronger together.

7. Keep Hope Alive: Even in your darkest moments, remember that hope exists. Hold onto it fiercely, for it is the light that will guide you towards healing.

As you finish reading this story, know that this is not an end, but a beginning. You are embarking on a continued journey of growth, healing, and self-discovery. Carry the lessons, the hope, and the strength you've found in these pages with you. Your story is still being written, and the most beautiful chapters may be yet to come. Keep moving forward, keep healing out loud, and keep spreading your light to the world

Epilogue:
The Journey Continues

As I write these final words, I'm struck by how far I've come — and how far I still have to go. Healing isn't a destination we reach and then stop. It's a journey that continues throughout our lives, bringing new challenges, insights, and opportunities for growth at every turn.

Since I began writing this book, my life has evolved in ways that continue to surprise and challenge me. There have been moments of profound joy, celebrating hard-won victories. But there have also been periods of struggle, when old wounds reopened, and shadows of the past tried to resurface. During these times, the lessons I've shared here have been my saving grace — embracing self-compassion, reaching out for help, and finding strength in vulnerability. Healing, I've learned, isn't about erasing pain or banishing it forever. It's about learning to live with it in a way that no longer defines or controls us. The darkness may creep in, but it no longer owns me. I've grown stronger in facing it and now have the tools to move through it.

As I've reflected on my journey, the lessons and tools I've shared here have evolved into the Aligned Liberation Framework—a philosophy born from my healing experiences. It offers a roadmap to transform pain into power and foster authentic connection, not just with ourselves but within our communities. While I've introduced its principles here, there is so much more to explore, which I'll share in my upcoming book. Healing doesn't happen in isolation; it's deeply intertwined with how we live, love, and connect with others. The Aligned Liberation Framework is not just a set of tools but a movement—a way of living that transforms how we love, connect, and heal. It's an invitation to step into freedom and authenticity while nurturing deeper connections in our lives and communities. I'll explore this further in my next book, inviting you to continue this journey with me.

Healing looks different for everyone. For some, it's about mending broken relationships. For others, it's about finding peace after loss, navigating unexpected life transitions, or reclaiming identity after trauma. Wherever you find yourself, the journey requires care, patience, and time. And that's okay. Your healing path is as unique as you are, and every step you take matters.

I've continued my work in mental health advocacy, speaking at conferences and workshops and sharing my story with others who are struggling to find their way. I've witnessed the power of breaking the silence around mental health — the relief in people's eyes when they realize they're not alone, the spark of hope when they hear that healing is possible. These moments remind me that vulnerability isn't just healing for ourselves; it's a gift to others.

In my personal life, my relationship with my son has deepened as I've opened up about my experiences. He's growing into a compassionate, emotionally intelligent young man, and I like to think my journey has played a part in shaping his understanding of mental health. Knowing that my healing has created a space for him to be vulnerable and free from the burdens of silence is one of my greatest joys.

It hasn't been all smooth sailing. There are days when the darkness creeps back in, and I find myself wrestling with familiar doubts and fears. But these setbacks have taught me resilience. They remind me that healing isn't about constant forward motion. Sometimes, it's about standing still and surviving the storm. Every step, even the hard ones, is part of the journey.

To you, dear reader, wherever you are on your path, remember that strength to move forward already exists within you. Healing isn't linear, but every step — even setbacks — matters in your growth. There will be difficult days, moments when progress feels elusive, but healing isn't linear. Every step, even those that feel like setbacks, is part of your growth. It's okay to feel lost or overwhelmed. What matters is that you continue to show up for yourself, no matter how hard it gets.

Keep reaching out. Keep practicing self-compassion. Keep believing in the possibility of healing. And above all, keep sharing your story. When we heal out loud, we don't just heal ourselves — we create space for others to begin their own healing journeys. Thank you for walking this path with me. It hasn't always been easy, but it has been worth it. Our journeys continue, and I'm honored to walk alongside you as we move toward healing and hope. There is so much more ahead — so many opportunities to grow, to love, and to live fully. Let's keep moving forward together, guided by courage, compassion, and liberation.

Closing with a Vision:
The Liberated Healed Self

Imagine a world where healing is not seen as a solitary endeavor but as a shared journey of growth and transformation. A world where vulnerability is celebrated, not shamed; where our stories of pain and resilience are embraced as powerful tools for connection and change. This is the vision of liberation—a state where each of us, no matter our past, has reclaimed the power to live fully, authentically, and unapologetically.

A Manifesto for Liberation

- **We Embrace Our Stories**: We honor every chapter of our journey, knowing that even the darkest moments have shaped the light within us.
- **We Speak Our Truths:** We refuse to be silenced by fear, shame, or stigma. Our voices are our power, and we use them to inspire others.
- **We Choose Healing Every Day:** Healing is not a one-time event but a daily commitment to self-love, self-care, and self-discovery.

- **We Break Cycles:** We confront the patterns and systems that perpetuate pain, creating new pathways of freedom for ourselves and future generations.
- **We Stand in Our Power:** We reject narratives that tell us we are not enough. We claim our worth and create lives that reflect our boundless potential.
- **We Create Ripples of Change**: Every act of healing — whether small or monumental — creates waves that extend far beyond ourselves, transforming families, communities, and the world.

My healing has been a gift to myself and others, creating space for reflection, connection, and growth. This is not just my story but part of a greater collective journey toward liberation. The journey doesn't end here. This is only the beginning of the life you are creating — a life rooted in authenticity, guided by resilience, and illuminated by the freedom to be unapologetically you. Together, as we heal out loud, we rewrite not only our own stories but also the narrative of what it means to truly live.

Your story is your power. Your voice is your liberation. Your healing is the beginning of something extraordinary!

Appendix
Meditations for Healing

As you explore these meditations, you'll find a space for reflection, renewal, and connection with your inner self. Find a quiet, comfortable place where you won't be disturbed. Sit or lie down in a relaxed position. Close your eyes and take a deep breath in, holding it for a moment, then slowly exhale. Repeat this breathing until you feel centered.

Healing Takes Heart

Emotional healing is the journey of transforming our pain into a source of strength and compassion. By embracing our feelings with love and understanding, we release the burdens of the past and open our hearts to joy and peace.

1. Focus on Your Breath: Breathe naturally, feeling calm and peace with each inhale, releasing tension with each exhale.
2. Visualize Healing Light: Imagine a warm, golden light surrounding your heart. Feel this light filling your heart with love, compassion, and forgiveness.
3. Healing Affirmations: Silently repeat these affirmations:

- I release all negative emotions and embrace peace.
- My heart is healing with each breath I take.
- I forgive myself and others, allowing my heart to heal.

4. Return to the Present: Bring your awareness back to your breath. Take a few deep breaths, feel the ground beneath you, and gently open your eyes, carrying the sense of emotional healing with you.

Clear Mind Bright Future

Mental healing empowers us to clear away the fog of negative thoughts and cultivate a garden of positivity and clarity. By taking control of our minds, we illuminate our path forward with resilience and purpose.

1. Focus on Your Breath: Breathe naturally, feeling calm and peace with each inhale, releasing tension with each exhale.

2. Clear Your Mind: Imagine a gentle breeze sweeping away any negative thoughts, leaving your mind clear and calm.

3. Healing Affirmations: Silently repeat these affirmations:

   - My mind is clear, calm, and focused.

- I release all negative thoughts and embrace positivity.
- I am in control of my thoughts and emotions.

4. Return to the Present: Bring your awareness back to your breath. Take a few deep breaths, feel the ground beneath you, and gently open your eyes, carrying the sense of mental clarity with you.

Body Renewal

Physical healing is an act of deep self-love, where we nurture our bodies with compassion and care. By visualizing and embracing healing energy, we honor our body's incredible ability to restore and thrive.

1. Focus on Your Breath: Breathe naturally, feeling calm and peace with each inhale, releasing tension with each exhale.

2. Visualize Healing Light: Imagine a warm, golden light surrounding any area of your body that needs healing. Feel this light bringing warmth, healing, and strength to that area.

3. Healing Affirmations: Silently repeat these affirmations:

- My body is strong, healthy, and healing.

- I am grateful for my body's ability to heal and regenerate.
- I nurture my body with love and care.

4. Return to the Present: Bring your awareness back to your breath. Take a few deep breaths, feel the ground beneath you, and gently open your eyes, carrying the sense of physical healing with you.

Soul Serenity

Spiritual healing connects us to our higher selves and the divine, guiding us towards inner harmony and purpose. By embracing our spiritual journey, we find peace and alignment with our true essence.

1. Focus on Your Breath: Breathe naturally, feeling calm and peace with each inhale, releasing tension with each exhale.

2. Connect with Your Spirit: Imagine a warm, golden light surrounding you, connecting you with your higher self and the universe.

3. Healing Affirmations: Silently repeat these affirmations:

   - I am connected to the divine and feel its healing presence.

- ○ My spirit is at peace and aligned with my higher purpose.
- ○ I embrace spiritual growth and healing.

4. Return to the Present: Bring your awareness back to your breath. Take a few deep breaths, feel the ground beneath you, and gently open your eyes, carrying the sense of spiritual healing with you.

Connection Harmony

Social healing strengthens the bonds we share with others, fostering understanding, empathy, and compassion. By visualizing harmony and connection, we create a supportive and loving community around us.

1. Focus on Your Breath: Breathe naturally, feeling calm and peace with each inhale, releasing tension with each exhale.
2. Visualize Connection: Imagine a network of golden threads connecting you to each person who supports you. These threads are strong, and they represent the bonds of love, friendship, and understanding. Feel the strength of those connections, knowing that even on your hardest days, you are never truly alone.

3. Healing Affirmations: Silently repeat these affirmations:

    o   I am surrounded by love and support.

    o   My relationships are healing and growing stronger.

    o   I communicate with kindness and understanding.

4. Return to the Present: Bring your awareness back to your breath. Take a few deep breaths, feel the ground beneath you, and gently open your eyes, carrying the sense of social healing with you.

Reader's Guide

1. In Chapter 1, Keana discusses the profound impact of losing her mother at a young age. How has loss shaped your own life? How have you navigated grief?

2. Throughout the book, Keana emphasizes the importance of self-love and self-acceptance. What does self-love mean to you, and how do you practice it in your daily life?

3. Keana's journey involves breaking free from toxic relationships. Have you ever had to leave a harmful relationship? What gave you the strength to do so?

4. The author's experience with bipolar disorder is a significant part of her story. How has this changed your understanding of mental health conditions?

5. Keana talks about the power of forgiveness, both for others and for oneself. What role has forgiveness played in your own healing journey?

6. The book emphasizes the importance of seeking help and building a support network. What barriers have you faced in seeking help, and how have you overcome them?

7. Keana's spiritual journey plays a crucial role in her healing. How has spirituality or a sense of higher purpose influenced your own life and mental health?

8. The author describes healing as a non-linear journey. How does this perspective change the way you think about your own growth and healing?

9. Keana's relationship with her son is a significant motivator in her recovery. How have your relationships influenced your mental health and personal growth?

10. At the end of the book, Keana emphasizes the importance of sharing one's story. How has reading about her experiences impacted you? Do you feel inspired to share your own story?

Resources

National Suicide Prevention Lifeline Call

1-800-273-8255 Available 24 hours every day

www.suicidepreventionlifeline.org

National Alliance on Mental Illness (NAMI)

Helpline: 1-800-950-6264 www.nami.org

Substance Abuse and Mental Health Services

Administration (SAMHSA) National Helpline:

 1-800-662-4357 www.samhsa.gov

Depression and Bipolar Support Alliance

www.dbsalliance.org

Mental Health America www.mhanational.org

Psychology Today (to find a therapist)

www.psychologytoday.com/us/therapists

Emotions Anonymous www.emotionsanonymous.org

Books:

- "The Body Keeps the Score" by Bessel van der Kolk
- "Loving What Is" by Byron Katie
- "The Gifts of Imperfection" by Brené Brown
- "An Unquiet Mind" by Kay Redfield Jamison

Apps:

- Calm (for meditation and sleep)
- Insight Timer (for meditation and mindfulness)
- Moodfit (for mood tracking and mental health tools)

Timeline of Healing

1999: Loss of mother at age 16

- Emotional turmoil begins
- Start of unhealthy coping mechanisms

2000-2002: Abusive high school relationship

- Diminished self-worth
- Deepening of emotional struggles

2002-2004: College years

- New environment brings hope and challenges
- Meet future wusband

2007: Birth of son

- The joy of motherhood was undeniable, but underneath, the emotional struggles still lingered.

2012: Marriage

- Increasing marital difficulties

2014: Father's death

- Unresolved grief compounds existing mental health issues
- Marital problems escalate

2013-2018: Infidelity and marital breakdown

- Deepening depression
- Feeling of losing control

2019: Suicide attempt

- Hospitalization

- Beginning of formal mental health treatment

2019: Separation from wusband

- Moving out on my own
- Struggles with independence and loneliness

2019: Start of intensive therapy and medication management

- Diagnosis of bipolar disorder
- Joining Emotions Anonymous
- Beginning of true healing journey

2020: COVID-19 pandemic

- Unexpected opportunity for self-reflection
- Deepening spiritual practices

2021: Divorce finalized

- Closure on a chapter of life
- Newfound sense of self

2022: Ongoing journey

- Maintaining mental health
- Advocating for others
- Embracing life with a new perspective

2024: Writing "Healing Out Loud"

- Using my experiences to help others
- Continued growth and healing

2025: Aligned Liberation Was Born

Practical Exercises

Self-Compassion Practice

1. Find a quiet, comfortable space.

2. Close your eyes and take three grounding breaths.

3. Place your hand over your heart.

4. Speak to yourself as you would to a dear friend who's struggling. Say: *"This is a moment of suffering. Suffering is part of life. May I be kind to myself in this moment. May I give myself the compassion I need."*

5. Repeat this practice daily, especially during challenging times.

Gratitude Jar

1. Every night before bed, write down at least one thing you're grateful for.

2. They can be big or small – from a beautiful sunset to a kind word from a friend.

3. Reflect on why you're grateful for each item. Place it in a Gratitude Jar.

4. On tough days, pull a note from the jar to remind yourself of positive moments.

5. At the end of the year, read through your notes and reflect on your experiences.

Emotion Mapping

1. Draw a simple outline of a human body on a piece of paper.
2. Think about a recent emotional experience.
3. Using different colors, shade in areas of the body where you felt that emotion physically.
4. Write words around the body describing the thoughts associated with that emotion.
5. Reflect on what this exercise reveals about how you experience emotions.

Values Clarification

1. Make a list of 10 values that are important to you (e.g., honesty, creativity, family).
2. Narrow this list down to your top 5 values.
3. For each of these 5 values, write down:
   o Why this value is important to you
   o How you currently honor this value in your life
   o One way you could better align your actions with this value

Healing Letter

1. Write a letter to your younger self at a time when you were struggling.

2. In this letter:
   ○ Offer words of comfort and understanding
   ○ Share wisdom you've gained since then
   ○ Express love and acceptance for who you were and are
3. Read this letter out loud to yourself.
4. Keep this letter and read it whenever you need a reminder of your strength and growth.

Cultural Context

Throughout my journey of healing and self-discovery, I've come to recognize the significant role that cultural factors have played in shaping my experiences with mental health and recovery. As an African American woman, my story is inevitably intertwined with the broader narrative of mental health in the Black community. It wasn't just my battles that shaped me but also the cultural expectations and stigmas that made seeking help so difficult.

Historically, there has been a stigma surrounding mental health issues in many Black communities. This stigma often stems from a complex interplay of factors, including historical trauma, systemic racism, and cultural norms that emphasize strength and resilience in the face of adversity.

The expectation to be a "strong Black woman" "fake it til you make it" or to just "pray it away" can make it challenging to seek help or even acknowledge mental health struggles. Growing up, I rarely heard open discussions about mental health. Depression, anxiety, and other mental health conditions were often dismissed as weakness or a lack of faith.

This cultural context made it difficult for me to recognize and address my own struggles early on. It contributed to my feelings of isolation and shame, as I felt I was somehow failing by not being able to overcome my challenges through sheer willpower.

Moreover, the lack of representation in mental health professionals posed another barrier. When I first sought therapy, I struggled to find a therapist who could truly understand my experiences as a Black woman. The intersectionality of my identity – being Black, a woman, and someone struggling with mental health – created unique challenges that not all mental health professionals were equipped to address.

However, my journey has also shown me the strength and resilience inherent in Black culture. The emphasis on community, faith, and perseverance has been a source of support and inspiration throughout my recovery. I've learned to reframe these cultural values in a way that supports my mental health rather than hinders it.

By sharing my story, I hope to contribute to changing the narrative around mental health in the Black community. I want to show that seeking help is not a sign of weakness, but a courageous step towards healing and self-empowerment. I believe that by speaking openly about our struggles and triumphs, we can create a more supportive and understanding environment for all those facing mental health challenges.

It's crucial to recognize that mental health support needs to be culturally competent and accessible to all communities. As we move forward, I hope to see more diversity in mental health professionals, more culturally tailored treatment approaches, and more open dialogues about mental health in all communities.

Remember, your cultural background is an integral part of who you are. It can present unique challenges in your mental health journey, but it can also be a source of strength and resilience. Embrace all aspects of your identity as you walk your path of healing.

Facing Systemic Barriers to Liberation

Healing is deeply personal, yet it doesn't exist in isolation. Our journeys are shaped not only by our individual experiences but also by the societal structures that influence how we see ourselves and navigate the world. These systemic barriers — whether rooted in cultural norms, economic inequality, or social stigmas — can inhibit our emotional liberation, making the path to healing more complex.

The Weight of Cultural Expectations

For many, cultural and societal norms dictate how we process emotions, often discouraging vulnerability or open discussions about mental health. Phrases like "be strong" or "don't show weakness" create environments where emotional struggles are hidden rather than addressed. This stoicism, while seen as strength, often reinforces emotional suppression and isolation.

Reclaiming Agency: Challenge these narratives by creating your own definition of strength. Strength isn't in pretending everything is fine; it's in acknowledging when it isn't and seeking the support you need. Surround yourself with individuals or communities that value emotional authenticity and encourage open dialogue.

Economic Inequality and Access to Resources

Financial instability and systemic economic inequities can create barriers to accessing mental health care, wellness resources, or even the time and space to focus on healing. Emotional liberation can feel like a luxury for those burdened by the demands of survival.

Reclaiming Agency: Liberation starts with small, intentional steps. Seek out free or low-cost resources, such as support groups, community workshops, or online mental health tools. Advocate for mental health accessibility in your community, and remember that healing doesn't always require professional help — it can also be found in moments of self-care, reflection, and connection.

Racial and Social Inequities

For marginalized communities, systemic oppression and discrimination create unique emotional challenges, often prioritizing survival over restoration.

Reclaiming Agency: Acknowledge the unique challenges you face without letting them define your healing journey. Embrace spaces that affirm your identity and provide safety for your emotional growth. Advocate for systemic change where possible, knowing that every step toward equity creates more opportunities for collective healing.

Breaking the Silence

Silence around trauma and mental health perpetuates cycles of pain. Family traditions, generational trauma, and societal stigmas often reinforce this silence, creating invisible barriers to emotional liberation.

Reclaiming Agency: Healing out loud disrupts this cycle. Sharing your story — whether publicly or within a trusted circle — shatters the silence and empowers others to do the same. By normalizing conversations about mental health and trauma, you contribute to a culture of openness and acceptance.

Future Outlook
The Aligned Liberation
Philosophy

What if every heartbreak, every setback, and every moment of disconnection weren't just obstacles, but stepping stones toward a life of true freedom, love, and connection?

After sharing my journey in *Healing Out Loud*, I came to understand that healing is not the final destination — it's the foundation for something greater. Healing transforms how we see ourselves, how we connect with others, and how we show up in the world. That's the promise of *Aligned Liberation*. As humanity moves into a new paradigm, the systems rooted in fear, control, and dominance are unraveling. This moment holds profound potential for transformation.

Aligned Liberation offers a framework to navigate this shift, helping us heal emotional wounds, dismantle toxic structures, and create a world where authenticity and freedom guide our lives.

The Core Pillars of Aligned Liberation

1. Emotional Safety: The Starting Point of Healing
    Healing begins where we feel seen, valued, and
    secure. *Aligned Liberation* emphasizes the need to
    create spaces — whether in relationships, families, or
    communities — where people can express their
    authentic selves without fear or judgment.

2. Self-Worth and Healing: Returning to Yourself:
    Anxiety, depression, and relational struggles often
    stem from unresolved wounds and diminished self-
    worth. *Aligned Liberation* invites us to reclaim our
    inherent value, confront our pain with compassion,
    and embrace healing as a return to wholeness.

3. Connection and Relational Empowerment: Thriving
    Together:
    Authentic connection is the cornerstone of thriving
    relationships. *Aligned Liberation* equips us to build
    bonds rooted in empathy, mutual respect, and
    emotional intelligence, transforming relationships
    into sources of nourishment and growth.

4. Raising the Global Vibration: A Collective Shift
    In this time of transformation, *Aligned Liberation*

encourages us to move from fear-based survival to love-centered living. By aligning our emotional, mental, and spiritual selves, we co-create a world rooted in empathy, authenticity, and shared empowerment.

The Ripple Effect of Aligned Liberation

Aligned Liberation is more than personal growth — it's about aligning our inner healing with a larger vision for our relationships, communities, and the world. As we heal ourselves, we contribute to a collective ripple effect of transformation.

- For those navigating anxiety and depression, it provides a foundation of emotional safety and self-worth.
- For those seeking deeper relationships, it offers tools to create connections grounded in mutual respect and authenticity.
- For those longing for change, it aligns personal healing with the collective transformation of our communities.

Through this philosophy, we break free from cycles of pain and disconnection, reclaim emotional sovereignty, and create lives where love, authenticity, and purpose thrive.

An Invitation to Liberation

Aligned Liberation is the next chapter in this journey — a philosophy that redefines how we love, lead, and connect. My hope is that as you move forward from *Healing Out Loud*, you carry the seeds of this movement with you, planting them in your life and the lives of those around you.

Together, we have the power to heal deeply, build authentic relationships, and dismantle toxic structures. By embracing *Aligned Liberation*, we co-create a future that uplifts and transforms us all.

Thank you for being part of this journey. This is just the beginning — the best is yet to come.

Glossary of Terms

1. Bipolar Disorder: A mental health condition that's deeply woven into my own journey. It's marked by extreme mood swings, from the emotional highs of mania or hypomania to the deep lows of depression. Living with bipolar disorder means navigating a constant balancing act between these two poles, learning to manage the unpredictability they bring.

2. Depression: More than just sadness, depression is a profound emptiness that can take over, draining life of color and meaning. It's a mental health disorder that makes even the simplest tasks feel impossible, and it's something I've had to confront head-on throughout my healing journey.

3. Anxiety: The ever-present knot in your stomach, the feeling that something is always about to go wrong. For many, including myself, anxiety can evolve into a full-blown mental health condition, making it difficult to find peace even in calm moments.

4. Trauma: Deeply distressing experiences that leave lasting marks on our mental, emotional, and physical well-being. Trauma is not just about what happens to us, but how those events shape who we are and how we move forward. In my story, it's a shadow I had to face in order to heal.

5. PTSD (Post-Traumatic Stress Disorder): A mental health condition triggered by experiencing or witnessing something terrifying. The flashbacks, nightmares, and severe anxiety that come with

PTSD were hurdles I had to learn to manage as I rebuilt my sense of safety in the world.

6. Cognitive Behavioral Therapy (CBT): A lifeline for many, CBT is a therapeutic approach that helps unravel the thoughts and emotions driving negative behaviors. It's been a crucial tool in my own mental health journey, allowing me to challenge the patterns that kept me stuck in cycles of pain.

7. Mindfulness: The practice of staying present, fully aware of your thoughts and emotions without judgment. Mindfulness became a key part of my recovery, helping me stay grounded when life felt overwhelming, and my mind wanted to drift into the past or the future.

8. Self-Care: Far more than a buzzword, self-care is an essential act of survival. It's the deliberate choice to prioritize your own well-being, whether through rest, reflection, or setting boundaries. In my story, self-care is what allowed me to rebuild from the inside out, honoring my needs for the first time in a long while.

9. Trigger: Something that brings painful memories rushing back, often without warning. Triggers are reminders of past trauma, and they've been a powerful force I've had to learn to recognize and manage during my healing journey.

10. Emotional Intelligence: The ability to understand, control, and express your emotions while also being

attuned to the emotions of others. Emotional intelligence has played a critical role in my growth, particularly in learning to navigate relationships with more empathy and self-awareness.

11. Resilience: The ability to bounce back from adversity. It's not about never falling; it's about getting back up, time and time again. My story is a testament to resilience — the toughness required to face life's hardest moments and keep going.

12. Stigma: The heavy weight of judgment society places on people with mental health conditions. It's the silence, shame, and misunderstanding that keeps so many from seeking help. Part of my mission is to break down this stigma, both for myself and for others who feel its burden.

13. Coping Mechanism: The tools we use — healthy or otherwise — to navigate stress and emotional pain. Over the years, I've had to re-evaluate my own coping mechanisms, letting go of those that harmed me and embracing new ones that foster growth and healing.

14. Dissociation: A disconnection from your thoughts, feelings, or sense of identity. It's a defense mechanism I've experienced during times of overwhelming trauma, and learning to stay present has been an important part of my healing process.

15. Gaslighting: A form of emotional abuse that causes you to doubt your reality, memory, or sanity. It's

something I've experienced in toxic relationships, and breaking free from it was key to reclaiming my sense of self.

Further Reading

For those wishing to dive deeper into the topics covered in this book, here are some valuable resources:

1. "An Unquiet Mind" by Kay Redfield Jamison A memoir that provides insight into bipolar disorder from both a personal and professional perspective.
2. "The Body Keeps the Score" by Bessel van der Kolk An exploration of how trauma affects the body and mind, and innovative treatments.
3. "Black Pain: It Just Looks Like We're Not Hurting" by Terrie M. Williams A powerful examination of depression in the Black community.
4. "The Gifts of Imperfection" by Brené Brown A guide to embracing vulnerability and imperfection.
5. "The Happiness Trap" by Russ Harris An introduction to Acceptance and Commitment Therapy (ACT) for managing difficult emotions.
6. "The Bipolar Disorder Survival Guide" by David J. Miklowitz A comprehensive resource for understanding and managing bipolar disorder.
7. "Reasons to Stay Alive" by Matt Haig A memoir about depression and anxiety that offers hope and humor.
8. "Self-Compassion: The Proven Power of Being Kind to Yourself" by Kristin Neff An exploration of self-compassion and its benefits for mental health.
9. "The Color of Hope: People of Color Mental Health Narratives" edited by Iresha Picot A collection of essays on mental health experiences in communities of color.

Websites and Organizations

- National Alliance on Mental Illness (NAMI): www.nami.org
- Mental Health America: www.mhanational.org
- The Trevor Project (for LGBTQ+ youth): www.thetrevorproject.org
- Black Emotional and Mental Health Collective (BEAM): www.beam.community
- The Loveland Foundation (therapy for Black women and girls): thelovelandfoundation.org

Remember, while these resources can be helpful, they are not substitutes for professional medical advice. Always consult with a qualified mental health professional for personalized guidance.

Acknowledgments

First and foremost, I thank God. His grace, love, and guidance have carried me through every storm and shown me that even in the deepest pain, there is purpose. Every word in this book and every step in my journey is because of His mercy and light.

To my beloved son, MaKyle: Your love is my anchor and my inspiration. You've given me strength in my darkest moments and joy beyond measure. I am endlessly proud to be your mother, and I hope my journey shows you the light you've brought into my life.

To the ones who see me in ways no one else ever has: You've given me the courage to speak and live my truth. Your presence has shaped this book in profound ways, and though your name isn't here, your spirit is in every chapter.

To my Wusband Michael: Our journey together has taught me invaluable lessons, and for that, I am grateful. Thank you for your patience, understanding, and the space you've held for me through it all.

To my late parents, my ancestors, and my guides: Your love, protection, and wisdom continue to shape me. You've lit my path in the darkest times, and I carry your presence with me always.

To my sister friends, my family, and my extended community: Your love has been my foundation. Thank you for your unwavering support, laughter, and honesty. You've lifted me when I couldn't lift myself, and for that, I am forever grateful.

To Miss Gwen: Your guidance has been a lifeline in my healing. Your wisdom and compassion have helped me see the light when I couldn't find it myself. Thank you for believing in me.

To Sway, Heather B., and Tracey G.: Your energy and positivity have inspired me to keep pushing forward and believe in the power of my voice. Thank you for your love and encouragement.

To my dog, Ali: Your companionship was a quiet comfort during my hardest days. I miss you deeply and cherish the love you brought to my life.

To my soulmates and everyone who has supported me: Thank you for walking this journey with me and creating space for vulnerability and truth. Your love has been a gift.

To those struggling with mental health, survivors, and those we've lost: This book is dedicated to you. Your stories matter. Your pain is real, and you are not alone. Healing is possible, and you are loved, needed, and worthy!

With endless gratitude and optimism for the journey ahead,

Keana

About the Author

Keana Shatteen is a courageous storyteller and advocate for mental health and emotional well-being. Her debut work, Healing Out Loud, emerges from the depths of her lived experiences, offering readers an unflinching exploration of grief, resilience, and transformation. Keana's journey from profound loss and trauma to self-discovery and liberation is a testament to the power of vulnerability, self-compassion, and finding strength through the cracks.

As a mother, survivor, and voice for those navigating life's darkest moments, Keana combines raw honesty with actionable wisdom. She writes for those who've ever felt silenced by their struggles, creating a safe space for readers to confront their pain and uncover their potential. Her personal experiences of loss, mental health challenges, and healing form the backbone of her writing, allowing her to connect deeply with audiences who yearn for understanding and hope.

When she's not writing or advocating for change, Keana enjoys traveling, spending time with her teenage son, family and friends, exploring nature, and finding solace in music. A Chicago native, she finds inspiration in the beauty of her surroundings and the connections she fosters through her work. Her writing is not just a story – it's a movement toward healing, growth, and reclaiming one's voice.